D1230372

THENFORD

For Annabel, Alexandra and Rupert

First published in the UK in 2016 by Head of Zeus Ltd

9 7 5 3 2 4 6 8

A CIP catalogue record for this book is available from the British Library.

ISBN (HB): 9781784979737
ISBN (E): 9781784979720

Edited by Mel Nichols
Designed by Paul Harpin

Photographs by Andrew Lawson, Clive Nichols, William Shaw,
Rupert Heseltine, Darren Webster, Marketa Hermova, Tate Images,
family & friends – and not forgetting Mr Dupe

Printed in Italy by Graphicom

Head of Zeus Ltd
First Floor East
5–8 Hardwick Street
London EC1R 4RG

WWW.HEADOFZEUS.COM

Michael & Anne Heseltine

THENFORD

The Creation of an English Garden

HEAD
of ZEUS

CONTENTS

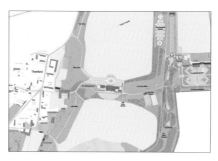

INTRODUCTION

WE ARE A NATION OF GARDENERS. Fascination with the colours and shapes of trees and plants stretches across the United Kingdom and embraces every social class. From the topiary of Tudor England, through the visionary landscapes of Brown, Repton and Kent to the more human intricacy of Jekyll and Lutyens, the stage set of our history has included gardens. From the armies of gardeners working on our great estates to the visitors who pay to view this inheritance, to the suburban acre, the street-side patch, or the neighbourhood allotment – we are all at it.

This book is the tale of just one garden and just one forty-year snapshot of that garden. It tells of the search for a family home, the challenges associated with the garden and the journey along which we converted the wild, overgrown and often dilapidated woodland surrounding it into seventy acres of ornamental features and perspectives, set amongst a significant collection of plants from many parts of the world.

Many people have travelled this way before but most of them in bygone centuries where the absence of cameras left their activities unrecorded. We have the advantage that we have kept a photographic record from the beginning. Some are no more than family snaps but, as time passed, we invited Britain's leading photographers to help us.

The ability to pay the bills has been essential to our endeavours. From the day we bought the estate, we have kept the immediate environs of the house as a private garden but the farm and most of the arboretum has been developed in conjunction with the substantial agricultural business and horticultural publishing activities of the Haymarket Group, which our family owns.

Anne remembers a remark that Michael made: 'I am now pretty rich. I don't have a yacht, or racehorses or any of those sorts of things – but I do have a garden.'

We would not have changed it for the world.

Michael and Anne Heseltine, Thenford, 2016

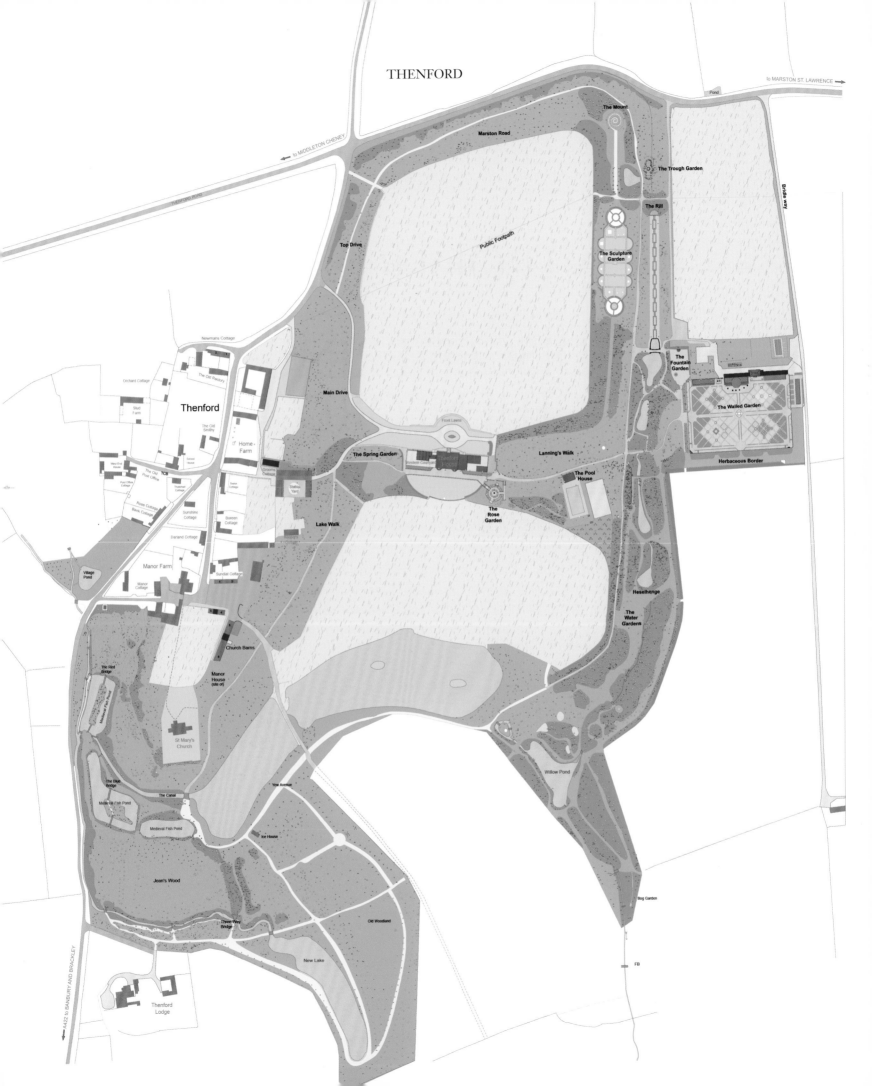

THENFORD

to MARSTON ST. LAWRENCE

to MIDDLETON CHENEY

THENFORD ROAD

Marston Road

The Mount

Pond

The Trough Garden

The Rill

Bridle way

Top Drive

Public Footpath

The Sculpture Garden

Newmans Cottage

The Old Rectory

Orchard Cottage

Thenford

The Old Smithy

Main Drive

Stud Farm

Home Farm

School House

The Fountain Garden

The Walled Garden

West End House

The Old Post Office

TCB

Post Office Cottage

Thatched Cottage

Grooms Cottage

The Spring Garden

Western Courtyard

Thenford House

Lanning's Walk

Herbaceous Border

Rose Cottage

Bank Cottage

Sunshine Cottage

Swan Cottage

Stable Yard

The Pool House

Boreen Cottage

Durland Cottage

Keeper's

Lake Walk

The Rose Garden

Manor Farm

Manor Cottage

Sundial Cottage

Heselhenge

Village Pond

The Water Gardens

Church Barns

The Red Bridge

Manor House (site of)

Willow Pond

Medieval Fish Pond

St Mary's Church

The Blue Bridge

Medieval Fish Pond

The Canal

Yew Avenue

Medieval Fish Pond

Ice House

Bog Garden

Jean's Wood

Three-Way Bridge

Old Woodland

FB

A422 to BANBURY AND BRACKLEY

New Lake

Thenford Lodge

Chapter One

DISCOVERING THENFORD

Michael said 'I think we may have found it!' The house felt welcoming and happy, and I knew that we could make this our home.

by Anne Heseltine

THENFORD
The Creation of an
English Garden

THIS IS THE STORY OF A BIG ADVENTURE, a search, and an arrival. A story of experimentation, disaster and – after mistake upon mistake – success!

Michael and I had been married for twelve years when we left our first constituency, Tavistock, in the West Country, in 1974. Michael had been elected its Member of Parliament in 1966. Tavistock is the biggest town on Dartmoor. Its surrounding moorland is full of tiny villages and farms, each a thriving entity with a personality of its own. We lived in a pretty house called Pamflete, near Holbeton on the Devon coast, where the woodlands ran down to an estuary that was alive with aquatic birds, and a deserted beach backed with high rocks. It was a paradise for small children – by then, ours were Annabel, who was eleven, Alexandra, eight, and Rupert, seven. Naturally, they did not want to leave and find a new home. But we were tenants, and the old constituency of Tavistock was being abolished. It had become imbalanced by the new suburbs growing up on the outskirts of Plymouth and it was hard for an MP to serve equally well constituents living an urban life, and those whose existence depended on farming. We had to

look for fresh fields. It was an opportunity. Ever since we had decided to spend our lives together, Michael and I had wanted a country house where we could make a beautiful garden, have land for our animals and enjoy privacy. And so our search began.

Our new constituency, Henley-on-Thames, in Oxfordshire, was in a particularly attractive part of the Chiltern Hills, covered in beech woods and rampant with bluebells and wild garlic in spring. It would reach its full glory in autumn when the beeches seemed to be on fire in all shades of red and yellow. It was also within easy commuting distance of London and nice houses were snapped up immediately, at very high prices. Our search for a home was all rather disappointing.

Suddenly, our luck turned. I had taken the children to Scotland for the Easter holidays and Michael was to catch us up a few days later. On the plane he sat beside David Fleming who owned a large house on the edge of the village of Nettlebed, a few miles from Henley, and several of the family – including Ian Fleming, the creator of James Bond – owned houses dotted about the area. David told Michael that he was proposing to sell his house, Soundess, in the hamlet of Crocker

Our first full view of Thenford.

End, because he was moving to Gloucestershire. He told Michael: 'It's the most hideous house in Oxfordshire but it's also in the most wonderful position, and a perfect place to bring up children. Come and see it, anyway.'

We enjoyed our holiday in Scotland, taking the children riding across the moors on fat, white, Highland ponies. Rupert perched on his like a flea on an elephant. When we returned to our house in London, Michael hadn't even mentioned his encounter with David Fleming – he was more than put off by the 'hideous' bit. But after a couple more houses were bought from under our noses, he finally fished from his briefcase an envelope that David Fleming had pushed into his hand as they'd left the plane.

Soundess really was rather ugly. It was 1920s Tudorbethan at its worst – a jumble of gables and beams galore. Anyway, we rang the Flemings and on a beautiful summer's evening we took the children with us to Crocker End. David and his wife Jocelyn wisely took us into the garden first, and told us the history of the place. Originally built in the fifteenth century, Soundess House had been the home of Nell Gwyn, mistress of Charles II. Local fables were endless. Dimly in the distance, beyond the hills, one could see the silhouette of Windsor Castle. It was as if no town or village lay between Soundess and the royal residence – they were all tucked into hollows along the route of the River Thames. The story went that Nell would light a beacon at Soundess, a sign that all was clear for King Charles to gallop across the hills to an assignation.

Behind the old walled garden – attractively built for the original house in typical Chilterns brick and flint – was a long, broad bank of earth, probably an ancient barrow. It was claimed to be Nell's burial place, and known locally as Nell Gwyn's Bower. A formal garden of roses was planted around a well where Nell was said to have thrown her jewels to protect them from the Roundheads. Alongside the main gates, up a long drive from Crocker End's village green, was a small stable block with a flat above and a red brick staff bungalow, somewhat charmless but practical and useful. Then, along what must have been the original tree-lined drive to the house, there was a pretty and productive orchard, two paddocks and a larger field on which we could make hay. In many ways, it fulfilled our requirements but we were certainly not in love with it.

The house itself lived up to its outward pretensions, with obviously modern-looking stained glass windows in the dining room and rather unlikely-looking linenfold panelling at every opportunity. On the other hand, the attics had been made into one large room which could house a ping pong table, Rupert's train set and all the other children's kit. A huge plus was the proximity of the Warburg Nature Reserve, a wonderful area of 300 acres of beech woods extending up to Maidensgrove Common, an open grassland where the children could ride in safety and we could follow the network of bridle paths that criss-crossed the hills. It was not ideal and certainly did not add up to the dream house we were seeking, but house prices were rising and we felt we should get on the ladder quickly. So we bought Soundess,

A print of Thenford House from John Bridges's *History of Northamptonshire* (1791).

knowing full well that we would probably move again at some point.

The children were very sad to leave Pamflete. No sea, no beach and no friends. But they settled down surprisingly quickly because Crocker End filled up at weekends with young families with children their age. They loved the beech woods, which offered them freedom and safety – although they soon developed a dangerous game, swinging on a knot of rope across a deep dell to Tarzan-like whoops of joy. Rather appropriate in view of their father's nickname, coined around this time.

But where next? And where were we to find a permanent home? We advertised – a half page in *Country Life:* A Palladian house, with land, condition unimportant because we were prepared to refurbish and restore with our own fair hands. This was all rather ridiculous and resulted in visits to near-ruins, several Victorian piles and other totally unsuitable houses. But it was fun: we were treated with great friendliness by owners and went to some beautiful places as well, but none really satisfied our desires.

We had started off with a wild dream. While staying in Suffolk with good friends Mark and Gabriella Schreiber (now Lord and Lady Marlesford) we had visited Heveningham Hall and fallen in love with its Palladian elegance and beautiful interiors by James Wyatt. We'd said nothing while we were there but back in London on Sunday night found that we had both been thinking 'this is it'. It was mad: wildly impractical for our lives, a long way from Westminster and with Michael the MP for Tavistock at the time, we had no idea whether it would be anywhere near a constituency that might fall vacant, and still less whether Michael might be selected for one. Nevertheless, we had rather unrealistic ideas about Michael quitting politics and using Heveningham as a base for a music festival – a possible link up with the Aldeburgh Festival? All pie in the sky! Michael was at the Department of the Environment (now the Department for Envi-

ronment, Food and Rural Affairs) which was trying to find a suitable use for the house. He was anxious to avoid any improper use of his position. Sadly, he had to stand back. But this image of perfection remained with us.

So we started on a new tack. Brazenly, we turned up large driveways and, if challenged, asked for 'Mr Wilkinson' before apologising profusely for having come to the wrong house and driving briskly back to the road. On one occasion, having been hoisted on Michael's shoulders, I looked over a promising estate wall. I was pleased with what I saw and we managed to get right up to the house and into the entrance hall. A group of rather sweaty young people in their twenties (so not a school) were coming back from a game of hockey. When we asked for Mr Wilkinson, to our horror we were directed to a corridor and told that his office was third on the left! We backed off hastily and said that we wouldn't bother him! We had invaded Heythrop Park, the then training headquarters of the National Westminster Bank.

In the summer of our second year at Soundess we took the family for a holiday in the Algarve. In our hotel we came across a delightful young woman, Kitten Summers, who, it turned out, taught the nursery class which Alexandra had attended at her London day school. While we were riding along the beach one day, she told us of a house that was being sold by a cousin whose father, Sir Spencer Summers, one-time MP for Aylesbury, had recently died. She said she would contact her cousin when she returned to England.

Back home, I went to the London Library to do some research. Could this be the same house that a Devon constituent had mentioned? She had said it was very beautiful and might soon be for sale because it had belonged to an MP relative of hers, who had died recently. I scoured the index to *Country Life* in the London Library, and skimmed through Pevsner's *Buildings of England* but found nothing of a house called Thenford in Oxfordshire. Frustrated, I telephoned Kitten Summers. 'Try Northamptonshire,' she said. 'The house is just on the border.' She was right, and I turned up two articles in *Country Life* published in the late 1950s. The illustrations showed a very Italianate house. It was set in rolling parkland but with virtually no garden, although there were some magnificent cedars surrounding the house. We decided to do a recce.

It was arranged that a Henley estate agent, Roderick Sargeantson, who had been helping with our search and had become a family friend, would come hunting with me when the Bicester and Warden Hill foxhounds were meeting near Thenford. Everything went right. The Master, Ian Farquhar, decided to draw a covert on a hill at the rear of the house. It was a perfect viewpoint. Thenford was a classic Palladian design and better than I had imagined. Its large, square, centre block had a double-hipped roof surmounted by a dome or lantern, with curtain walling leading to two smaller buildings at either end. Frustratingly, we could not view the house from any other angle but had seen enough to know that we might be nearing the end of our search.

Michael and I set forth one Saturday with the children and

The view on Anne's day with the hunt.

Roderick. An ex-Blues and Royals soldier, Roderick was almost a caricature of a Guards officer – impeccably groomed and dressed, but game for anything. This immaculate figure joined Michael to crawl through the thicket of elders, hollies and sycamores on either side of the drive while the children and I kept watch from the car on the narrow lane outside.

After an anxious twenty minutes or so, Michael and Roderick emerged covered in leaves and twigs. There was a grin on Michael's face. 'I think we may have found it!' he said. But how could we progress further? The house was not officially on the market and we did not want to pester the recently widowed Lady Summers with the importunate letters we had written to other owners of likely houses. So once again we asked Kitten for advice. Through her, we contacted Martin Summers, who had inherited the house. He was extremely helpful and arranged for us to have lunch with his mother, Jean. She was an elegant, imposing and extremely likeable lady, and seemed to approve of us. Like her late husband Sir Spencer, Michael was an MP; like her, we had three children; and we were interested in wild birds, and enjoyed riding and hunting. After lunch, I had a splitting headache but Michael went off with Lady Summers and Martin to see the rest of the estate – about 400 acres, farm buildings, a walled garden and a very pretty village with cottages built in the honey-coloured, locally quarried, Hornton stone. Left alone in a large, unknown house, I could have been rather daunted but it felt welcoming and happy, and I knew that we could make this our home.

Lady Summers was obviously very sad about leaving Thenford, where all her children had grown up. She moved into Thenford Lodge, a large Victorian house in the southwest corner of the park. She retained the nearby lake, a chain of silted up mediaeval fishponds and twenty-five acres of adjacent woodland – later to be known as Jean's Wood – on the understanding that we would eventually buy her or her heirs out. The contract was drawn up in the summer of 1976 and we were given vacant possession for the spring of 1977 so that the Summers family could spend one last Christmas there.

We moved in on Whit Friday. As we listened to the radio among the packing cases, Red Rum won the National for the third time on the Saturday, and life at Thenford started for the Heseltine family.

Thenford is near the southwestern border of the straggling county of Northamptonshire. When we came to live here I was surprised that so little was known of its history. I began to explore the county – the south in particular – and especially the delights of the Record Office in Northampton, whose then librarian was recommended by Lady Juliet Townsend. Juliet, granddaughter of F. E. Smith (Lord Chancellor 1919-1922) and later to become the county's Lord Lieutenant, had written *The Shell Guide to Northamptonshire*. She helped me immensely.

Northamptonshire is known as the county of 'Spires and Squires'. Almost every village boasts a sizeable manor house or hall, usually sitting beside a parish church of almost cathedral-like proportions that seems incongruous with its small rural community. The pastureland is particularly rich in minerals and, through the wool trade, helped bring vast wealth to the seventeenth and eighteenth century squirearchy both before and after the Enclosure Act. It is now widely ploughed but the dense hedges remain, the farmers are still comfortably off, and many fields provide grazing for the hunters and the National Hunt 'jumpers' that thrive in this part of the Midlands. Several villages can boast a Grand National runner, and horses are still the folk heroes here.

The Romans were the first to colonise Thenford – the Oxford University Archaeological Society excavated a substantial Roman farmhouse here in 1971. Then came the Saxons, who formed the Kingdom of Mercia, of which this county was a part. When the Mercians declined in about AD 800, the kingdom was added to the monarchy set up by Egbert the West Saxon. It was later seized by the Danes who, according to county historian John Bridges, 'wasted the country about them with fire and sword'. At the time of the general survey made for the Domesday Book in 1086, there were thirty Hundreds (administrative divisions) in the county, one of which was Sutone or Sudtone Hundred in which lay the hamlet of Taneford.

The Domesday Book's entry for Taneford/Teworde shows that there was a mill, and the main tenants in the village were Roger from Robert d'Oilly and Mainou le Breton who held land 'from the King'. The Manor of Thenford eventually descended to Sir Thomas Cheyne in the fourth year of the reign of Henry VII. By his wife, Anne, Sir Thomas had an only daughter, Elizabeth, who, in the sixth year of Henry VIII's reign, inherited the manor. After her father's death, she married Lord Vaux of Harrowden. Her son from this marriage, William Lord Vaux, sold the manor to Fulk Wodhull Esq in 1565. He subsequently styled himself Fulco de Thenford and, according to *The History and Antiquities of Northamptonshire, compiled from the Manuscript Collections of the late, learned Antiquary, John Bridges Esq., by the Rev. Peter Whalley* 'is supposed to be the person who lies buried in the arch within the north wall of the Parish Church... he is reported to have lived an hundred and four years. But this tradition is without foundation, for it appears both by the Parish Register, and the inquisition taken upon his death, that he died in 1613, the eleventh year of James I, and consequently could not have been above 83 years old at the time of his decease. The fourth in succession from him is John Wodhull Esq. the present Lord of the Manor of Thenford'.

Thenford now has fewer dwellings than were recorded on an Ordnance Survey map showing tithe-free land in 1851. But there is a unity of architecture and all are built in Hornton stone. It is a surprisingly sleepy village despite its proximity to the busy market town of Banbury, with its modern industrial estates, just five miles west. Residents remember that there was once a shop, a public house, a post office and even a school. Only the post office has left a legacy: a letter box built into the thickness of its wall, and a white painted sign that said *Thenford Post Office* which adorns what is now Post Office Cottage. The Old Schoolhouse has been renamed The Old House even in the forty years we have lived here.

The Roman farmhouse's site exposed.

Fulk Wodhull.

Detailed workings.

Village folk *c.*1860.

Head of Ceres in the mosaic floor.

St Mary's Church.

St Mary's, the thirteenth century church, has a service once a month. Worshippers walk across a paddock to make up the sparse congregation. The rectory has been a private house for many years and the parish is part of a benefice with six churches. Even non-church-goers love the church and help to decorate it at Christmas or Harvest Festival. It is tiny but entirely unspoilt. It rests alongside the site of the original Thenford House, which was built in mediaeval times and refurbished during the reign of Elizabeth I. It was then demolished when the existing house was built in 1760.

Michael Wodhull, the affluent young landowner who built it, was typical of his breed of country gentlemen. He lost as much money at Northampton Races as any man but his intellectual and cultural aspirations set him apart from others. His modest house – modest, that is, by the standards of other Northamptonshire houses such as Easton Neston, Boughton or Aynhoe Park – is worthy of a brief history in the context of this book.

Wodhull (or Woodhull – he used both versions indiscriminately) built his Palladian 'house on the hill' between 1760–65 to provide a fitting and elegant setting for his famous library and print collection, and as a place to pursue his studies. He did not employ an architect but based the design of the house on patterns from The British

Architect by Abraham Swan. The book had been published recently in London and Philadelphia for the benefit of the new settlers there. Swan was the architect of a nearby house, Edgecote, and we know that Wodhull and the then occupants were friendly. Michael Wodhull first saw a painting by Johan Zoffany at Edgecote. It inspired him to commission Zoffany to paint a portrait of his wife, Catherine or Kitty, as Flora, the Goddess of Flowers and of Spring. The painting is now in Tate Britain. Catherine Woodhull, in her draped classical garments, looks slightly uncomfortable as Flora but comes across as a typical English lady gardener with a trug full of plants, including the recently introduced *Passiflora*. One can easily imagine her at work with her trowel or deadheading the roses.

Like so many of the landed gentry of his day, Michael had crossed the intellectual barrier between affluent country living, farming, racing and hunting and that of the cultured gentleman. Sadly for us, he doesn't seem to have been much of a gardener although he must have had someone to guide him because the new concept of landscaping did not pass him by. There are substantial stone ha-has on both sides of Thenford House, which extended the views across the landscape without the interruption of a wall or a hedge. Perhaps that was Kitty's influence.

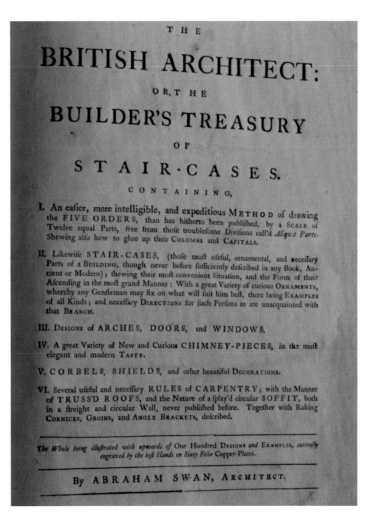

The old housekeeper photographed by W. H. Dupe.

The British Architect by Abraham Swan.

Michael Wodhull's tomb.

Catherine died childless in 1808 and Michael set off to Paris to see the great libraries and console himself. It had obviously been a happy marriage despite the lack of children. But it was a bad time to travel abroad and he was imprisoned in the Bastille on suspicion of espionage. His health was undermined and after his return to England he died in 1816. The Thenford estate then went briefly to his sister-in-law, Mary Ingram. We know little of her except that she suffered a theft from her garden in August 1818. I once had a telephone call from a local priest who needed money for his church. He said he had an item that he thought would interest me. I was intrigued and invited him over. It was an advertisement that read: 'Ten Guineas Reward… a Person or Persons entered the garden belonging to Mrs Ingram and stole thereout, a quantity of Cucumbers, about 2 bushels of Onions, about 5 dozen of Apricots…' I couldn't resist and gladly paid the price he asked.

At Mary Ingram's death, the estate went to the Severne family. Samuel Amy Severne had been an old school friend of Michael Wodhull and his family would continue to own the property until 1934. Luckily, the Severne's main home was in Shropshire and Thenford was not much visited. As a result, it was not altered from Wodhull's original plan and suffered none of the unlovely additions that were

MICHAEL WODHULL ESQᴿ

Michael Wodhull was famed for his library.

Above The ad the local priest sold Anne. *Right* Catherine by Johan Zoffany.

frequently imposed on similar houses in the Victorian era.

Michael Severne was the last of his family to live at Thenford. His mother died when he was only a small boy and he was raised by the woman who became his stepmother and bore his father a second son. The children found themselves fatherless as schoolboys and the young mother, nervous about running a large estate, decided to sell Thenford and invest the proceeds for the two boys. The entire place sold for £10,000 during the 1930s depression and so there was little left when the boys came to manhood. Notwithstanding, Michael had a successful career as a manufacturer of modern furniture. Later, he inherited the beautiful house Shakenhurst in Worcestershire which had belonged to another branch of his family.

Michael visited us several times at Thenford and was delighted by our mission to bring the house and estate back to its former glory. In a series of very fruitful and enjoyable meetings, he brought me a treasure trove of sepia photographs taken in the 1860s by the then butler at Thenford House, a Mr W. H. Dupe. Dupe left service to become a full time photographer but not, thank goodness, before he had had time to record the village and inhabitants of Thenford. He won awards – one at a competition in Switzerland for a picture of the 'Bathing Pond' at Thenford, easily identifiable as the lake below the church. Generous-

ly, Michael Severne lent me these photographs, gave me spares, let me copy anything I liked, and said that when he died he would make sure I was given the whole album because it belonged at Thenford. Sadly, though, after his death in 2007, the album could not be found but fortunately I have a good collection of the photographs. Some of them are in this book.

When we bought Thenford, we were delighted with the village which, uniquely, contained no eyesores; no nineteenth or twentieth century horrors! However, there was work to be done. We noted that many of the roofs were exceptionally steep, built so that the rain would drain off them easily. This was an indication that they had originally been thatched, because the steep pitch is unnecessary for a tiled roof. We decided to restore the thatching to any cottages that lent themselves to this treatment. We used reeds rather than straw because it is much more durable, and long straw, suitable for thatching, was hard to get in England at the time and often had to be brought over from Holland or Scandinavia.

Next to the Home Farm on a central location in the village – then a patch of brambles and elder, occasionally used as a dumping ground for weeds and rubble – there had once been the old smithy. We decided to rebuild it, and did so by basing it on old photographs kindly

The prize-winning photograph 'Bathing Pond' taken in the 1860s by W. H. Dupe.

All that remained of the old smithy.

provided by Michael Severne. Further up the lane, just past the Old Rectory, was a rather unlovely building used as a potato store. This, too, called out for work. Here again, Michael Severne's photograph of it as a cottage, with the owner at the front door, proved invaluable during the subsequent rebuilding. This redoubtable lady, Mrs New-man, turned out to be the grandmother of the old gentleman who owned the first supermarket in nearby Middleton Cheney, and still attended church in Thenford, as a nod to his ancestry. He was thrilled to have a copy of the photograph. I send up a little prayer for Mr Dupe, the butler who so often solved a problem for us through his portrayal of the village and its inmates in the 1860s onwards. If only every village and district had been chronicled so carefully.

The next cottage that deserved our attention was Manor Farm cottage. Very small, very pretty, it had been the home of Betty, Lady Summers's cook. When she and her husband left to live in a care home, we gave it to Annabel, our eldest child. By this time, Annabel, a successful journalist, was living a very independent life and needed a weekend refuge where she could entertain her own friends or catch up on some much-needed rest. The cottage was in dire need of re-furbishment: the sky could be seen through the roof at one end, and poor Betty had decamped to the small kitchen at the other end, with a

A thatched house in the village *c.*1860 captured by Mr Dupe.

Thenford village *c*.1860.

Mrs Newman at her door in the 1860s.

By the 1970s her house was a potato store.

The old smithy rebuilt.

Mrs Newman's cottage today...

...and from the southern end.

Posing in the stableyard for W. H. Dupe's camera *c.*1860.

Betty's cottage under repair.

staircase leading to a tiny bedroom. After the builders left, it was very comfortable, with two small bedrooms, a long bedroom which also served as a playroom, and two small living rooms downstairs. This cottage was also reroofed with thatch. The garden had been Betty's pride and joy, well-tended by her husband – only known as Watts – but sadly, the builders had to invade it with their machines and building materials and it was a sorry sight after their departure. The proud survivor was a topiary peacock, perched unscathed on the yew (*Taxus baccata*) hedge. Annabel soon put the garden back to rights, although she and her husband, Peter, moved on shortly after their marriage because it was not really right for a rapidly expanding family. They moved into Manor Farmhouse, when the farmer, Mr Goodwin, retired, and completely revamped it. The tractor shed became their kitchen/dining room. Again, Annabel created a pretty garden: she seems to have inherited Michael's passion.

The stableyard, located between the village and the house, we found to be large: loose boxes built down one side, carriage houses

Below Coach and horses arriving for the meet.

Above Children near original pond. *Below* The wires criss-crossing the village that we had removed.

down another and, on a third side, garages which presumably had at one time been hay stores. The original hay loft had been adapted for use as a village hall. We were desperately short of living space for staff in our early days because Lady Summers had wished her pensioners to stay in their original tied cottages so the village hall became two small flats. Since we rebuilt the Church Barn to be used for village purposes, they have stayed that way. The fourth side of the square yard was the wall of the garden of Keeper's Cottage, where our groom and family have lived for some years. The original groom's cottage was known as The Bothy, and was tacked on to the range of carriage houses. It was tiny, and even then had lost one room to tack. We decided to enlarge the cottage, and move the tack room into one of the carriage houses. We made a circular grassed area in the middle of the yard, and planted a few trees. Just outside the yard gates was a barn which served no particular purpose but when I decided to breed horses in the 1980s, it made comfortably spacious foaling boxes. We don't know how the yard looked originally, although we have some charming photographs by Dupe of the Severne's carriages in it.

I said there were no eyesores in the village but the twentieth cen-

Village pond now...

...and as it was.

tury had done its work in bringing the convenience of electricity. The wires were like a cat's cradle. Michael did a deal with the local electricity suppliers, who buried most of them, and transformed the look of the place.

Towards the lower end of the village, near Thenford Lodge, there was a mess. Overgrown willows (*Salix spp.*) and, in the spring, a sheet of snowdrops (*Galanthus spp.*) grew out of a boggy area on the opposite side of the lane. Pretty in spring, the bog virtually dried up in the summer but was fed again in the autumn by a tiny stream. Unbelievably, this had once been the site of a watermill, which had been working as recently as the 1920s. It was the last transformation within the village on our list. Now, we have a duck pond, with a grass surround, and a few trees placed around it. The ducks are yet to arrive but they will, although we fear their numbers may be depleted by the local foxes. But it's worth a try.

When Lady Summers died in 1995, and Thenford Lodge became ours, it lay vacant for some time. A large house, we felt that it would not be easy to let, and that a possible solution would be to convert it into two or three flats. But we were reluctant to do that. It would have

Above Thenford Lodge *c.*1900. *Right* The Old Avenue.

spoilt the house, which is a very fine example of its era. Fortunately, the perfect, unforeseen answer to this problem arrived. Our younger daughter Alexandra had married Nick Williams and they had been house hunting in the area for some time without any luck. They came to us one day (they were weekending in the Home Farm house at this point) and asked if they could have it. We were relieved and immediately offered it to them. Nick wanted, understandably, to feel that it was his house, so they bought it. They have done a magnificent job. It is now exactly as it should be, with furniture and paintings of the period. Nick has been able to express his passion for all things Pugin, and Alexandra has covered the walls with the works of William Strang. The old stable block has become Alexandra's gallery, where she has exhibitions of drawings and paintings two or three times a year.

The Summers family became tenants of Thenford briefly before the Second World War, during which it was occupied by an evacuated boys' prep school. The Summers returned to purchase it in 1948. They then broke up the estate, selling off the outlying farms and only retained 440 acres. We have steadily re-expanded by buying back

Chinner Farm, Stanwell Farm, some surplus land from the Chacombe golf course, Middleton Farm and a further 250 acres that stretch from the Home Farm to the village of Farthinghoe. We also acquired the glebe lands and various fields nearby as they became available. As recently as 2014 we purchased seventy acres of land from local farmers on the other side of the lane from the Lodge.

An old avenue across the fields from the main A422 Banbury-Brackley road was the original driveway to Thenford House. It had been cobbled and, when the hunt goes down it, you can hear the horses' hooves pounding on the stone. There were trees on either side but many had died. The farm's hedgerows had been planted with elms but Dutch Elm Disease had decimated them. Pathetically, young trees reappeared only to die at about ten to fifteen feet. We replaced them with oaks (*Quercus spp.*) and horse chestnuts (*Aesculus hippocastanum*). Some of the hedges had grown out of hand – sometimes up to twelve feet – and clumps of elder (*Sambucus nigra*) had taken over. These were replanted with hawthorn whips (*Crataegus monogyna*) and are now thick and effective.

Above The southern façade in the twentieth century. *Below* Michael Wodhull's plantation.

As we returned the estate to a commercial scale, we also began to replant the woodlands. Apart from a few ornamental bridges that had more or less disintegrated, the Walled Garden was the only trace of any gardens there might have been in the eighteenth century. It is a quarter of a mile to the east of the house and its stone-capped brick wall encloses roughly two acres. Since the 1920s the wall has been interrupted by a cottage where our Head Gardener, Darren Webster, lives. Built in 1926, the cottage had been cheaply made, with ugly metal windows and a white-painted stucco render. Over the years, we have restored the Walled Garden and reworked the cottage into the attractive dwelling it is today.

An old gardener who worked on the estate in the 1920s and 1930s told me that at that time all work around the house had to be completed by nine a.m. Then the gardeners retired out of sight into the glasshouses and Walled Garden while their employers strolled unimpeded around the shrubberies and lawns. So far away, indeed, was the active garden within the walls that a pony pulling a little cart was employed solely to transport the vegetables and flowers back to the kitchens.

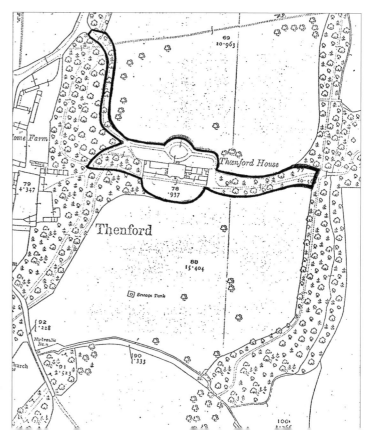

Above A cedar that fell in the late 1990s while Anne and Darren watched. *Next page left* Alison Crowther's cedar memorial. *Right* 1851 OS map of Thenford.

Nowadays a golf buggy does the job – not so romantic!

The rear elevation of Thenford House is much less grand than the formal front. Curiously, too, it appears far smaller, principally be-cause the two wings are almost masked by the red brick walls that screen the service courtyards. One wing houses the estate office, and the other a drying yard from the days when the right-hand wing was a laundry. This wing has now been transformed by the classical archi-tect Quinlan Terry into a two-storey library and its courtyard planted up – difficult because there is little light there. It is a quiet place to read a book.

In many ways, the rear of the house is the most sympathetic as-pect. A horseshoe-shaped croquet lawn with a castellated yew hedge – planted in the early twentieth century – is bordered by a ha-ha above the parkland which then slopes down to the valley and the lake. Two immense bronze cormorants by Guy Taplin stand silhouetted against the lake. At either end of the croquet lawn, opening from the gravel walk along the house, are cast iron gates made in Coalbrookdale in the Ironbridge Gorge, Shropshire, in the nineteenth century.

The whole house is encircled by Michael Wodhull's plantation, a narrow strip of woodland whence the old beeches (*Fagus sylvatica*) and limes (*Tilia* × *europaea*), once its main feature, are now mainly gone. It was the need to replant this that led to the start of the arboretum.

Ancient cedars (*Cedrus spp.*) shelter the house, although the winds of 1986 tore one of them badly and the best and most beautiful one died ten years later. I was coming back from a walk with the dogs when I saw Darren standing beside this great tree. He was listening intently. I sensed that something was wrong. I dumped the dogs hastily inside the safety of the courtyard and stood beside him. The tree gave out a deep groan, an anguished moan of pain, and sank to the ground in a dignified manner, slowly and almost silently. As it fell, its side branches supported it on the ground. When it finally came to rest it looked like some great monster or dinosaur with many legs. It was a great sadness to see it go, but its time had come. Later, we wanted a memento of this magnificent tree so we asked sculptor Alison Crowther to carve its timber into abstract cone-like shapes that sit on the gravel path to remind us of our lost giant.

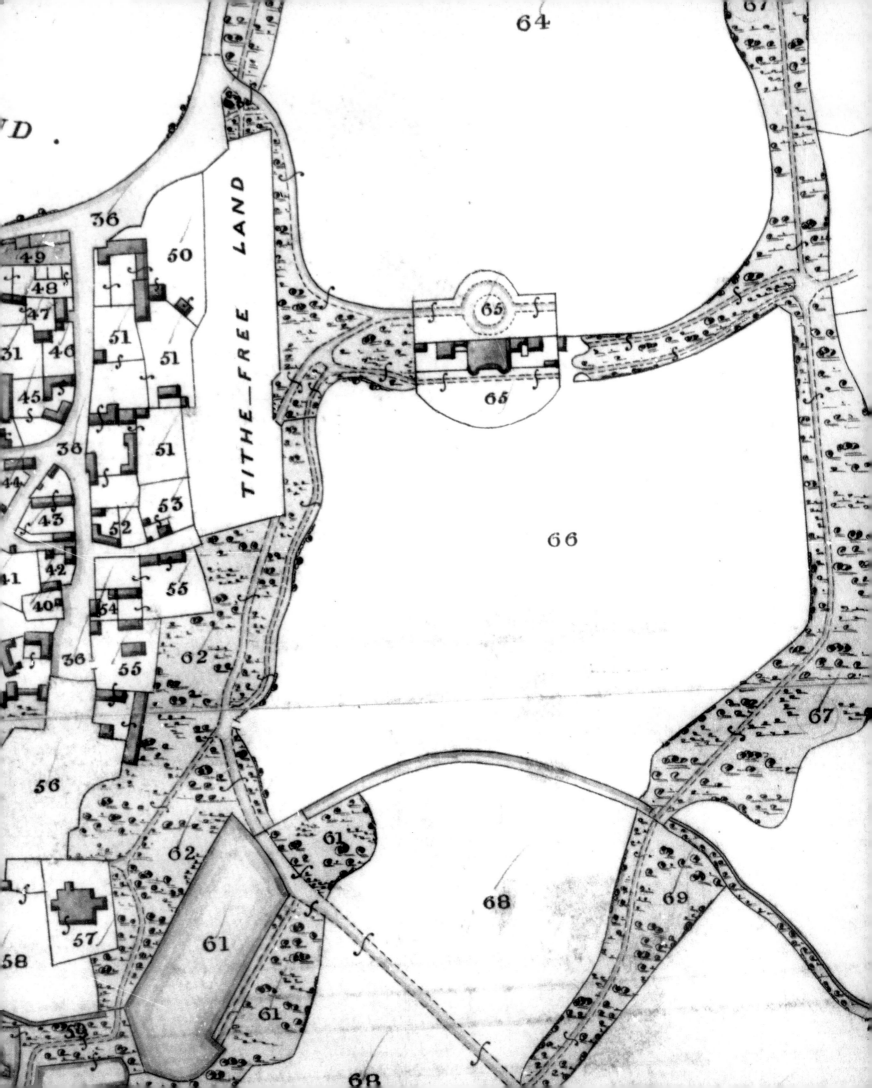

Chapter Two

HOW WE BEGAN

After an overambitious start and a series of frustrating mistakes, a plan begins
to emerge with the help of revered designer Lanning Roper.

by Anne Heseltine

THENFORD
The Creation of an
English Garden

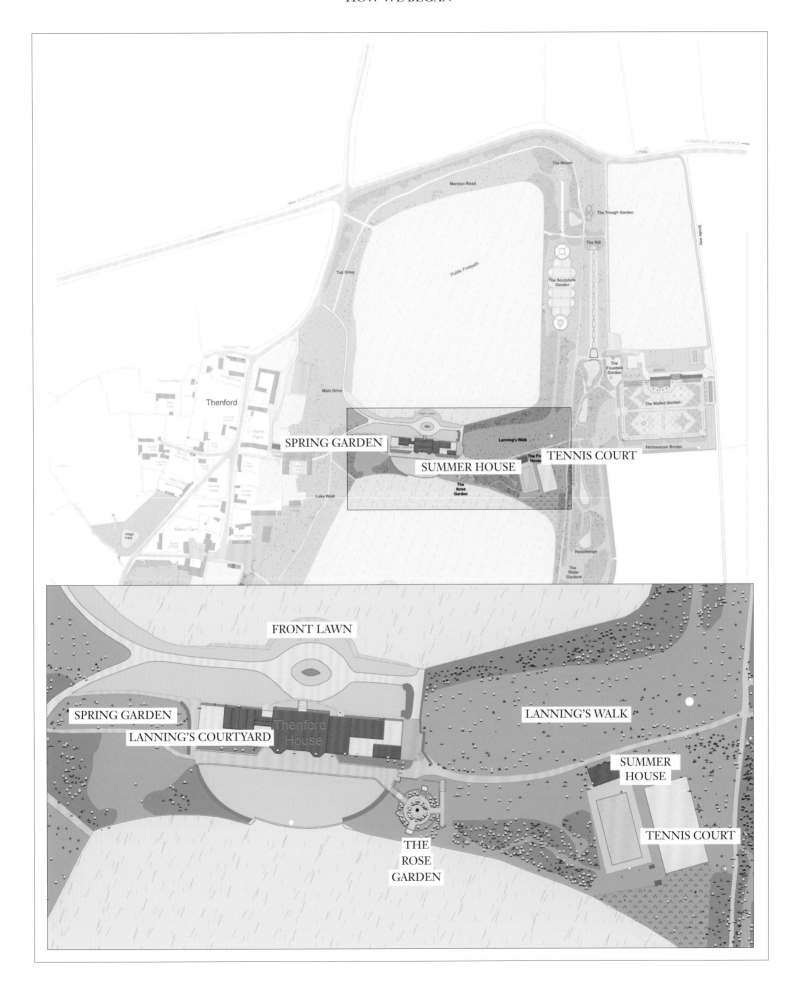

WE HAD A LONG WAY TO GO TO reach the garden of our dreams – not that we had a very clear idea of where we were going. We were overwhelmed by the amount of space at our disposal and we had no master plan.

One of our first projects must have looked like an extra and was hardly gardeners' work. It was a swimming pool. When the children said goodbye to their beach in Devon we promised them they'd be able to continue swimming. We built a pool as a matter of priority at Soundess and vowed to do the same at Thenford. The design of both pools was identical – a Y shape with shallow steps leading down from the arms of the Y into the pool – because we had worked out this was safest for young children. We planted a yew hedge around the pool to protect it from the wind. We really were greenhorns: we had imagined that the yew hedge would be a ten-year project and were amazed and delighted by the speed at which it grew. This encouraged us to extend the original yew hedges in the garden and to replace those that had become old and straggly. We later discovered how quickly yew recovers if it's cut back hard in the spring. The land was not flat, so a

wall and steps led onto an upper lawn where we planned eventually to have a summer house. The Summers had planted a small English oak (*Quercus robur*) there. Lady Summers begged us to retain it. We did, and that sapling is now about sixty feet high.

We were rather uncertain about the design of our Summer House. Michael had been attracted by Niemeyer's Ministry of Foreign Affairs in Brasilia and felt that the Summer House should be entirely contemporary and as adventurous as Thenford House itself had been when Michael Wodhull built it. However, we sounded out the feelings of the local planning authorities and were advised that we would never get planning permission on that basis. Since we had renovated the house and excluded some later additions – mostly modern windows which intruded on the original design – it had been upgraded from Grade 2* to Grade 1, and the restrictions were much tougher. Michael was Shadow Secretary of State for the Environment at this time and asked his colleagues for their advice about a classical architect. Quinlan Terry's name emerged. Although still quite young, Quinlan had already made a name for himself with his designs for country houses

Our first swimming pool.

in the Palladian style and, after the death of his partner and mentor, Raymond Erith, he was head of his practice in Suffolk. He came to visit us and we immediately found a rapport.

Each spring for several years I had visited the tiny spa town of Abano in the Veneto, northern Italy, famous for its mud baths. I had spinal problems and found the baths very beneficial. The treatments took place in the early morning to avoid the heat of the day, leaving much time to explore. I had visited most of the wonderful villas built around the Veneto by Palladio. The town of Vicenza wasn't far from Abano. Palladio designed its famous theatre and many of its noble houses. Quinlan was familiar with them all and had made meticulous drawings of these great classical buildings, which were his inspiration.

We chose a position near the swimming pool for the Summer House that is approached through a gate from the long border. Quinlan suggested that he design an orangery, with a large chimney piece so that we could be warm in winter; two changing rooms with showers; and a small kitchen and storeroom. It is a triumph! It's useable in all seasons, wonderful for village parties at Christmas, sublime for

summer lunches on a windy day – and on a very hot day we can escape the wasps. A friend with multiple sclerosis who cannot cope with stairs has spent the night there in the summer, with the fire well-stocked with logs. He woke to see a deer grazing on the lawn outside.

The exterior of the Summer House was based loosely on an orangery in the garden of a Palladian villa in the Veneto. We built it mainly of Hornton stone from the last of the quarries on the far side of Banbury but the dressings and pinnacles on the roof are of Clipsham stone. They are an attractive contrast: while Hornton is mainly gingery with a blue-grey streak running through it, Clipsham is a warm creamy colour. Quinlan designed the alternating pilasters with Composite and Corinthian capitals – the latter, he felt, were suited to Michael's personality. I never delved more deeply into this! The interior has a vast fireplace and the floor an exciting geometric pattern, in grey slate and a whitish stone. That left the walls unadorned, and Quinlan suggested that they should reflect the frescoes, as in one of Palladio's buildings.

About this time, Annabel met a young man, Marcus May, who

Setting for sublime summer lunches.

Marcus May's wall decorations.

had decided that the Army was not where his future lay, and was planning to leave at the end of his present term. When she brought him to Thenford on a visit, he greatly admired the plans for the Summer House and mentioned casually that he was thinking of becoming a professional mural painter. I asked him whether he had ever painted any. Rather to my surprise, he replied affirmatively. So I went to London to see a friend's house where he had painted a small hall. I was very impressed and rather ashamed of my scepticism. I spoke to Quinlan about him, and we decided to give him a go. We expected to see a plan on paper but Marcus arrived with brushes and paints, ready to start work.

After some discussion with Quinlan, it was decided that the architect would design the *trompe l'oeil* architecture but that Marcus would design and paint two trophies on either side of the chimneypiece, two views on the end walls and medallions around the cornice with portrait heads of Michael, me and the three children. We left two medallions blank, for Rupert's wife, and possibly the next heir, if he had a son. This didn't quite work out: when, in due course, Rupert married

Sarah, she wisely pointed out that she was not marrying a ten-year-old boy as portrayed, so the medallion remains blank – perhaps for a portrait of William, their now thirteen-year-old son when, as we hope, he eventually lives at Thenford.

The finished decoration is a triumph: one of the trophies was painted from the one designed for Roy Strong's exhibition The Garden at the Victoria and Albert Museum in London. It is made up of garden tools sprayed white. The other was formed from gear in our gun room – fishing and hunting impedimenta. The final touch at the base of one of the garden views is a small squirrel perched on a balustrade, tearing up and devouring the notes written by Lanning Roper, our first garden designer! I should add that Marcus May is now a very successful artist who not only produces murals but has painted many country houses and their estates.

Some years later, the little garden in front of the Summer House was redesigned by local designer Carolyn Cumming. We trained wisteria on the curved walls either side of the house, white (*Wisteria brachybotrys* 'Shiro-kapitan') on one side and blue (*Wisteria sinensis*) on

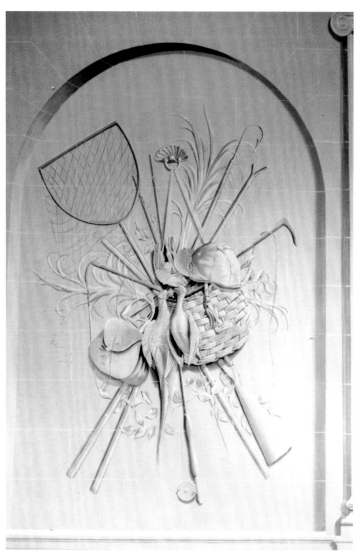

Marcus May's wall decorations: gun room...

...and garden tools.

Our Summer House above the original pool.

Quinlan Terry's Summer House façade.

the other. We introduced curved stone seats and pots of the brightest summer plants we could grow. I found some nineteenth century iron coal scuttles from Belgium in a junkyard. Suitably repainted, we planted them up and placed them in front of the windows. We also planted another yew hedge with a sinuous line, and two pillars and two obelisks of yew after buying two metal frames from a local blacksmith, Culworth Forge, to ensure we achieved the shape we wanted. They made the upper lawn an entity so that one was not always aware of the purely functional pool below. Since then, the pool has been redesigned in a classical shape and with a black interior so that it looks like natural water. The great interior designer David Hicks suggested this but sadly, by the time his idea was implemented, he was no longer alive to see it. It has a more efficient heating system now, and a solar cover to save energy and reduce heating costs. I found in the West Country a statue of Neptune leaning on his trident and he now reigns over this watery area from a niche in the hedge.

Initially, the Summer House was used for teas when the garden was open. I coped with the catering myself in the beginning, with

White wisteria on one of the curved walls.

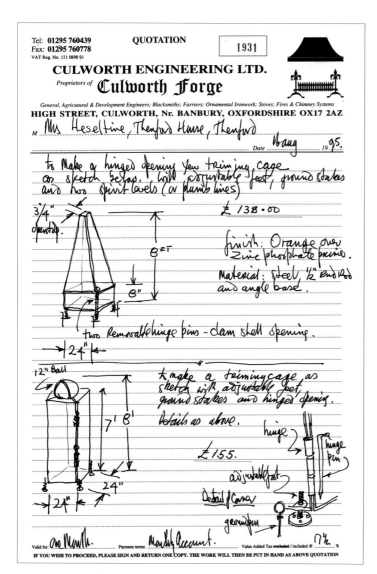

Culworth Forge's costing for the yew frames.

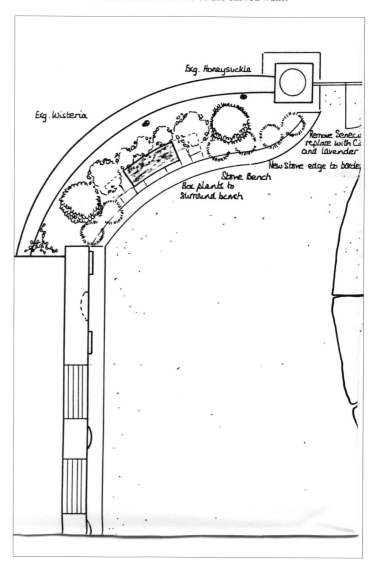

Carolyn Cumming's design.

the help of family and friends. But our daughters went to boarding school and the numbers swelled – we opened up on four days a year and the several hundred visitors needed a more professional approach. We had bought the remains of Manor Farm, in the village, when its owner retired. It included a fine barn with a central storage area for hay and straw, and cow byres and milking parlours at either end. We converted the central area into a facility with a kitchen, loos, and a cloakroom. The storage space, with a new roof, central heating and stone slab floor, can seat 100 at round tables, or 150 in rows. We do the teas – kindly run by the village ladies – for garden visitors there now. The proceeds go to cover the costs of maintaining our beautiful church and its churchyard. Apart from its commercial role, the barn serves as a focus for the village. The old cow byres at either end are now two decent-sized cottages for gardeners.

Next to the swimming pool garden was a somewhat battered tennis court. Obviously unused for some years, it was full of potholes and its netting sagged to the ground. On the low surrounding wall, grass snakes sunbathed happily, disappearing into crevices if the weather was bad. It needed a rethink but we didn't want to spend a lot on it so we brought in a team of itinerant road repairers to tarmac it and replace the netting, and found it quite adequate. Later, we had it professionally surfaced by En-Tout-Cas but by then bad knees and creaky backs had removed our zest for tennis and, really, we'd had more fun on the old tarmac.

While we lived in Devon, we visited a constituent who had a collection of wildfowl that we admired and coveted. When we first saw Thenford, one of its attractions had been the lake. We knew it would make a home for waterbirds. But when Lady Summers decided not to include it in the sale we had to think again. Between the house and the Walled Garden was an area crammed with laurels which we decided must go. A broken-down bridge with gates at either end crossed the laurel patch. Michael and I decided to start hacking down the laurels from either end and meet at the bridge. I couldn't see him from my end but I heard him calling: 'Hi there, my feet are in water!' I looked down at my wellies. I was in a couple of inches, too. We walked towards each other and realised that we were on the bed of a stream.

Neptune in the yew hedge below the pool.

The barn makes a fine tea room.

The ugly aviary fence.

LABOUR LEADER 'SHOULD SUSPEND DEMO COUNCILLORS'

Blair pair vandalised Hezza's garden

By Chris McLaughlin

TARGET: Michael Heseltine

TWO protesters who vandalised Michael Heseltine's lawn were last night unmasked as Labour councillors.

Gerald Johnson and Jane Hackworth-Young joined a gang of environmentalists and miners in a lawn raid on the Deputy Prime Minister's house last week.

Last night an angry Mr Heseltine challenged Labour leader Tony Blair to order the suspension of the two councillors. 'Mr Blair preaches about the need for better standards in public life. He should start by looking at the activities of his own public representatives,' he said. 'People in public life should not be allowed to behave like common vandals.'

In an echo of the Tories' anti-Blair campaign, he added: 'New Labour, new moles — and that is before they start on your taxes.'

The revelation that the two are Labour councillors comes at the end of a week in which Mr Blair called for a return to traditional family values as the basis for new moral standards and behaviour in society.

An unrepentant Mr Johnson said he would be prepared to repeat the protest against open-cast mining.

RAID: Hackworth-Young

Shovels

Insisting the action did not conflict with his position as a councillor in Hammersmith and Pulham, West London, he said: 'It's something that I'm not ashamed of and if it came to it I'd do something similar again.

'If he wants to fill in the hole, Mr Heseltine had better roll up his sleeves and do it himself.'

During the protest, about 50 pheasants escaped — to certain death in the wild — from a coop in the grounds.

Mr Johnson, 48, a retired biologist, denied any knowledge of birds being freed and claimed reports that at least one of them had already died were 'vicious rumour-mongering'.

In the Miners' Support Group Associates raid along

UNREPENTANT: Johnson

with Mr Johnson and councillor Hackworth-Young — also from Hammersmith and Pulham — was social worker and Labour supporter Peter Turner.

Led by Arthur Scargill's wife Anne, they blame Mr Heseltine for closing down pits and opening the way for open-cast mines which are said to scar the countryside. The protesters, carrying shovels and pickaxes, marched on Mr Heseltine's Palladian retreat of Thenford Hall in Northamptonshire, dug up the turf and sank a borehole in the front lawn.

Mr Heseltine revealed that he had been rearing pheasants for about 15 years and that they were worth around £30 each.

The birds cannot survive in the wild and one has already been found dead, probably killed by a fox.

'By releasing them you are condemning them to a slow death by starvation or by foxes,' said Mr Heseltine.

DIGGING IN: Protesters armed with shovels and pickaxes dig up Mr Heseltine's lawn

Scouts get the Old Left to fall in line

SCOUTS have scored a victory over their local council's 'Old Labour dogma'.

The 89th Reading Scouts were appalled to have a request for a £300 tent turned down because the Labour-run council had ruled no grants would be made to 'uniformed organisations'.

Opposition councillors called the decision 'political correctness gone mad', while Scout group leader Dr Chris Corti branded it 'totally unfair and unreasonable'.

Following an appeal by senior councillors, the scouts will get a one-off payment under grants available to community groups for training or equipment.

Dr Corti said: 'I'm convinced part of the original decision was about old Labour having suspicions of Scouts being middle class and Tory.'

How the press covered the demonstration.

We carried on for half a mile or so and knew that this area had the potential to become a water garden. That was extremely exciting – but proved to be very hard work and not something that we could do unaided because at this stage we had very few support staff. Michael and I worked hard, tearing out self-seeded shrubs and digging up roots, freeing the little stream to run over the gravel and stony bed. But at that time he was a minister who had to snatch time where he could. I had three children, school runs, cooking and a large house to run and refurbish.

Eventually, we cleared the stream. With the help of contractors armed with mechanical diggers we created five ponds and put up a high wire fence to enclose about two acres to house our waterbirds and game birds. The top of the fence was bent backwards at an angle to stop foxes getting into the area where the birds would be. The first inmates began to arrive – a fascinating collection of swans, geese, ducks and exotic pheasants. The pheasants were our first mistake. In the breeding season, their flamboyant plumage at its best, the Golden pheasants and Lady Amherst's fought for supremacy and sired somewhat ragged looking mongrels. The large collection of superb waterbirds were nearly all fathered by farmyard Muscovies, kindly but unwisely given to Michael as a birthday present by the children. We had kept the foxes at bay but had quite forgotten about overhead marauders. Hawks, magpies, jackdaws and crows attacked the eggs and dined off the fledglings. Squirrels dropped off overhead branches for a quick snack of corn from the hoppers. Later, any young birds that had survived were susceptible to rodents who dug their way under the wire netting.

We were faced with humiliation – but were somewhat cheered when we lunched with Sir Solly Zuckerman, President of the London Zoological Society, at London Zoo. We recounted our tale of woe and he invited us to view the Zoo's collection of wildfowl. Thinking we were about to be shown perfectly bred examples, we were delighted to see much the same collection of crossbreeds that we had produced at Thenford. It's hardly surprising that our ardour as aviculturists was losing its appeal, overtaken as it was by our ambitions for the Walled Garden. In October 1996, within a month of Darren Webster's arrival as a young graduate from the Royal Botanic Gardens, Kew, he had to cope with the consequences of the coal mine closures. A small group of demonstrators vandalised the swimming pool boiler room, released the pheasants from their cages and, in a bravura gesture to their political affiliation, planted a scarlet thorn (*Crataegus laevigata* 'Paul's Scarlet'), in our south park. Abiding by the adage that you should never look a gift horse in the mouth, we carefully replanted it in the arboretum where it continues to flourish. Only three of the pheasants were

A fascinating though troublesome collection.

Brown and blue eared pheasants.

Eider duck.

Whooper swan.

Black swan.

White peacocks.

The massive roots of the centuries-old ash.

recaptured and then given away. The cages were later cleared to make space for autumn borders.

Apart from the fact that the aviary had looked so awful, another swift lesson we'd learned was that webbed feet and marginal planting are impossible partners. Without the birds we could plant the margins extensively. But that meant controlling the invasive natural plants that are far more aggressive than our more decorative cultivars. Later, when we built our third lake, we had lengthy discussions about the marginal planting with an environmental officer. He had in mind his favourite natural vegetation. We wanted to preserve the option of more exotic planting. It was quite a sterile conversation. Nature moved in and did the job for us.

The area between the Water Gardens and the Walled Garden – about an acre – had once been an orchard and was approached by a bridge over our north-to-south stream, Marston Brook. The trees were now old and gnarled and, left unpruned, barely produced a half dozen apples apiece. The glory of the orchard was a very old and very tall ash (*Fraxinus excelsior*). Its huge roots spread out over the surface of the grass, and it was here that we began our snowdrop collection. We divided different varieties neatly between the prominent roots that acted as enclosures. There was also a very productive walnut tree (*Juglans regia*), so heavy with fruit that it had to be propped up with

Michael and Anne on the ash's roots.

42

The orchard in April.

Cowslips within the ash's roots.

Across the path primroses and grape hyacinths abound.

a crutch. Sadly, it fell and split during the great winds of 1986. The ash continues to prosper and, after the snowdrop season, provides a dramatic stage for sculptor Laura Ford's 'Armour Boys' – tragic little figures in armour, young squires and pages, dead and dying, some maimed, some apparently asleep, inspired by the scene described by King Henry V after the battle of Agincourt. I was worried that Annabel's children might be upset by the sight of them when they were walking around the garden. We concocted a story in which some little boys had dressed up in armour and after playing a battle game had gone to sleep from sheer exhaustion. I need not have bothered. Mungo, the oldest, came running back to tell me: 'Granny, Granny, they're not asleep – they're all dead!' And, licking his lips: 'One of them has had his arm cut off!' I always knew that children were bloodthirsty; even Mungo, normally a gentle child.

The snowdrop collection was Michael's new passion. It was one I did not share – much as I love snowdrops *en masse* and enjoy visiting Snowdrop Valley near Wheddon Cross, Exmoor, every year. There, they grow on the steep banks of a heavily wooded valley, spread like snow on the grass. But I have never seen the point of paying £25 or more for a single bulb that can only be distinguished from its more common neighbour by lying on one's stomach on wet, cold ground and peering at the green dot that marks it as 'rare'. I found a fellow

sympathiser. We had given lunch to a group of galanthophiles in our barn. Afterwards, they were rushing around the gardens excitedly, armed with cameras and notebooks, recording every obscure variety. I saw one lady head up a path away from the snowdrops and ran after her. 'I am afraid there are no snowdrops up this path,' I said, and was surprised by the answer: 'Thank goodness! I never want to see another snowdrop again.' We walked around happily together looking at early flowering shrubs and rejoined the galanthophiles for tea.

The Spring Garden, a shrubbery opening from the west side of the house through a pair of Coalbrookdale gates, was a revelation when it came into its prime soon after we moved in. In the late summer, when we had first seen the house, it was a rather uninteresting mass of green shrubs with a few larger trees which bordered a path through to the stableyard. But in the spring it was a non-stop extravaganza. First came the snowdrops and then the aconites (*Eranthis hyemalis*), then its paramount moment when the sapphire anemones (*Anemone blanda*) flowered with their startling blue, everywhere, that lasted for several weeks. Next came daffodils (*Narcissus spp.*) and more blue with grape hyacinths (*Muscari spp.*) and bluebells (*Hyacinthoides non-scripta*) canopied over with the magnolias (*Magnolia spp.*) – we hold an extensive collection of more than 200 species and cultivars; see also Chapter Four). The grand finale was a sea of frothy white cow parsley

Left An 'Armour Boy' near the ash. *Above* The Spring Garden in all its glory.

One of the 'Armour Boys' against the ash's roots.

Above Martagaon lilies. *Next page* The Spring Garden in bloom.

Left The Spring Garden in winter. *Above Corylopsis spicata* add colour to the border.

(*Anthriscus sylvestris*) interspersed with martagon lilies (*Lilium martagon*) before it all quietened down and was mown to a rough green lawn. We established shrub borders to either side which included spike witch hazel (*Corylopsis spicata*), creating something of an amphitheatre once we had finished clearing, with a view down to the new lake.

Lanning Roper, a famous designer whose work we had admired in the gardens of Pat Gibson and Prue and Eric Penn, came to help us about this time. Lanning was also the gardening editor of *The Sunday Times*. Pat, then Chairman of the National Trust, recommended him wholeheartedly.

Shortly after we exchanged contracts to buy Thenford, Michael had phoned Lanning, explained that we had just bought a 400-acre estate and a listed house and would much appreciate his professional advice. Michael thought it seemed a very attractive offer and expected an immediate and favourable acceptance. Far from it. 'I must be frank with you,' Lanning said. 'I simply can't take on any more work. I'm too busy. Ring me in a year's time.' He probably assumed that that would be the end of it. A year later, Michael phoned again and the conversation was predictable. 'You told me to ring today,' Michael said. 'You will remember what I said a year ago; I hope now you are able to accept.' To our immense satisfaction the answer this time was 'yes'. Later, there was a possibility that Lanning would contribute to the gardens at Highgrove soon after the Prince of Wales had bought

it from the Macmillan family. But Lanning had become unwell and had decided that Thenford might be less demanding than Highgrove – how wrong he was!

When Lanning had looked at our garden for a while he became worried that we wanted to run before we could walk, and that our huge aspirations could never be fulfilled, particularly in view of the few staff we then employed. He would have been surprised and delighted to know that we now have ten gardeners! I saw a lot of him. He always arrived at Thenford on a Friday and did a day's work, planning, drawing and taking notes, before Michael returned from his constituency on Friday evening. Lanning had to put up with me and the children for Friday lunches. He always included the children in the conversation and conspired with them to find surprise presents for Michael's birthdays – always useful, and always (unsurprisingly!) gardeners' toys. When he was in hospital with what proved to be terminal cancer, I was particularly touched when he sent me a large box of regal lilies (*Lilium regale*) with a card saying, 'For Anne, to whom we did not always listen enough'. Sadly, he died in 1983.

Lanning's signature plants were lady's mantle (*Alchemilla mollis*), lavender (*Lavandula spp.*), Labrador violet (*Viola labradorica*) and *Rosa* 'White Pet' and its white companion *Rosa* 'Wedding Day'.

I can still hear him saying their names lovingly in his soft American accent. The Library Courtyard is still known as Lanning's, and the

The large wispy panicles of *Cotinus* 'Flame', stunning in autumn. *Next page* Flowering cherry near the Summer House.

long border up to the Sculpture Garden as Lanning's Walk. He was always the most wonderful guest even in his time of declining health when, as he said, his 'climate control' had failed him and he would be swathed in scarves and jerseys at lunch in our centrally heated dining room or walking around the garden in shirt sleeves when we were in our Barbours.

On the other side of the house, running down to the swimming pool and tennis court, was a double herbaceous border protected by a long cotoneaster (*Cotoneaster sp.*) hedge on the field side. This was all replaced by a shrubbery, but leaving a wonderful flowering cherry behind which we built the swimming pool. Nearest to the house was a rose garden: beds were laid out like the rays of the setting sun and planted with floribunda roses. Lanning changed the design to concentric beds, with an Istrian wellhead from Venice as a centre point. To my delight I was given the task of planting it up. Lanning advised me to use wild rose species (*Rosa spp.*) because they were better suited to our soil. I enjoyed choosing these early roses and discovering their origins. Some that were brought by Crusaders returning from the Holy Land had been carried along the Silk Route to the Middle East centuries before. They were tough and needed little pruning or pampering. Best of all, they were unmucked-about-with, smelt absolutely intoxicating and had a long flowering period. A visit to Mottisfont Abbey, near Romsey in Hampshire, was invaluable; it has the National Collection. So was Peter Beales's book *Classic Roses* for researching their history and description. We underplanted the roses with lavender but sadly that wasn't a success. Thirty years later the rose bushes were huge and straggly and the lavender had all but disappeared. I longed to have Lanning around to tell me where I had gone wrong. Perhaps more judicious pruning?

It became clear that a rethink of the Rose Garden was necessary. But I will tell you all about that in Chapter Eleven.

The Rose Garden as it was.

Chapter Three

FIRST PROJECTS

A visit to the Sir Harold Hillier Gardens brings happy consequences – the inspiration

for our arboretum and Harold's invaluable advice about what to plant where.

by Michael Heseltine

THENFORD
The Creation of an
English Garden

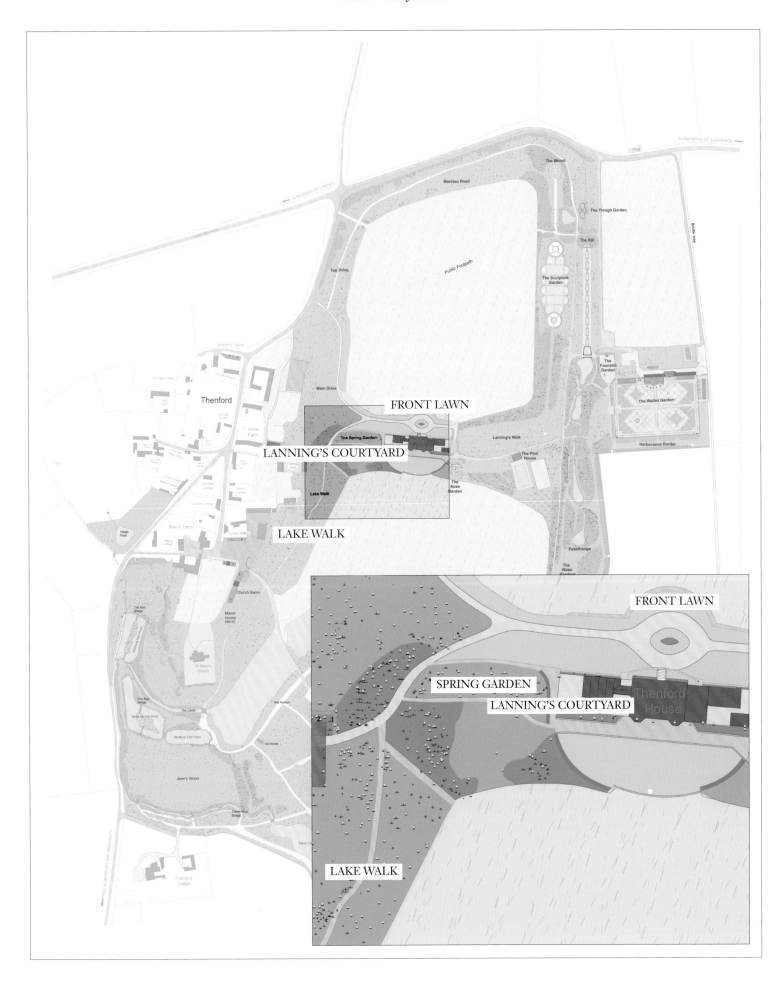

DURING OUR SEARCH FOR A COUNTRY HOUSE we had assumed it would have a garden. In the event, Thenford House was in the centre of a horseshoe-shaped woodland of about twenty-five acres but had only a very limited formal garden surrounding it. Below the western side of the house there were another twenty-five acres that included the mediaeval fishponds and a one-and-a-half-acre lake which had been created we're-not-sure-when. It had been used as a bathing pool in the nineteenth century, with its changing hut and boathouse built in one corner. They must have been very stalwart in those days: most of the water is permanently in the shade and is therefore cold. St Mary's church, standing alongside the lake, is a perfect eye-catcher when you see it reflected in the water.

Before we arrived, there had been little or no maintenance for decades. The only recent planting, so far as we could tell, had taken place in the 1920s when the young Michael Severne and his brother were told by their father to plant ash saplings nine yards apart in different places, including a small clearing alongside the lowest fishpond. Old trees remained where they had fallen, like sticks in a giant's game of spillikins. It was wild, unkempt, fascinating, charming and of great nostalgic value to our predecessors, particularly Jean Summers. Of

Lanning's Courtyard as it was.

course there is another way of looking at it: here was a massive opportunity for us to replant and restore.

The fishponds and the canal that fed the lake were so silted up you could walk across them. The only way to identify their location was by the shallows in the soil and the rushes. Very handily, the 1851 Ordnance Survey map that Anne found in the Northamptonshire Record Office showed the outline of the original ponds. In the drought of 1976, the year we bought Thenford, the bathing lake shrank to a small pool about six inches deep at the centre of the reed beds, willow banks and stretches of mud into which neighbouring sycamores (*Acer pseudoplatanus*) had tumbled.

So what was our great plan? Where was the vision? In truth, neither of us was equipped to answer these questions and, in many ways, had we tried to grapple with such detail, the cost might have caused us to abandon the project.

That is not to say that we weren't enthusiastic. I had been a keen gardener since I went away to school at Broughton Hall in Staffordshire at nine years old. One of my first memories is of the headmaster, George Thompson, giving each boy a square yard of mud and a packet of Virginia stock seeds (*Malcolmia maritima*). Meticulously I spread my seeds. A few weeks later I was mesmerised by a dazzling variety of colour. At that moment, my love for gardening was born.

In 1945, when I was twelve, my parents bought a substantial house with a two-acre garden on the outskirts of Swansea. Restoring it and maintaining it absorbed their energies and encouraged my interest. Wherever in our married life Anne and I have lived, traces of this enthusiasm emerged – but herbaceous borders and vegetable plots are one thing; trees and shrubs within an arboretum quite another.

So if there was passion but no plan, where were we to find help? In Chapter Two, Anne mentioned my phone call to Lanning Roper. He was the first professional to whom we turned. When he arrived in 1977, it was to the areas close to the house that he devoted his attention.

He redesigned the western courtyard early in our friendship. We had some difficulty persuading a family of fancy pigeons that their owners had moved a mile away and they were expected to follow. Their cage was demolished but they hung around for weeks. Lanning used the shade inside the long southern wall for four varieties of osmanthus – *Osmanthus delavayi, serrulatus, heterophyllus* and *heterophyllus* 'Purpureus' – interspread with *Viburnum tinus* 'Bewley's Variegated', *Choisya ternata, Fatsia japonica, Mahonia × media* 'Charity' and *Mahonia × media* 'Buckland'. A slope in the ground was removed by creating two levels linked by stone steps between two stone obelisks set to view a weeping white mulberry (*Morus alba* 'Pendula'). Camellias and roses grow well on other walls and nowadays the beds rotate with bulbs, wallflowers (*Erysimum spp.*) and tobacco plants (*Nicotiana sylvestris*).

We moved a large, lead eighteenth century cistern bearing Michael Wodhull's initials and the date of Thenford House – 1765 – from the front of the house to a more appropriate place against the courtyard's eastern wall. Originally, it would have been in a courtyard

Lanning's Courtyard's first redesign looking west...

...and as its plants begin to mature.

The rare and pretty *Pyrus amygdaliformis* var. *cuneifolia* on the front lawn.

but had been shifted to the centre of the elliptical lawn in the drive outside the house's north entrance.

Lanning's immediate focus was on the lawn to the front of the house. He proposed very simple planting. The original buttress of golden yew (*Taxus baccata* Aurea Group) at the east end of the lawn made a perfect background for a glorious pear tree (*Pyrus amygdaliformis* var. *cuneifolia*). We planted two pairs of golden yews (*Taxus baccata* 'Fastigiata Aureomarginata') to frame the house. Now nearly forty years old, they need topping, as historian, curator, writer and garden designer Roy Strong has strongly advised. He is quite right. These are big trees and their branches have gradually spread from their early tight formation. (There's a very interesting example of what happens if you leave them to grow in Tom Hudson's yew avenue at Tregrehan, near St Austell in Cornwall.) Finally, Lanning placed a red oak (*Quercus rubra*) and a tulip tree (*Liriodendron tulipifera*) on the top of the ha-ha, and added a bird cherry (*Prunus padus*) and a white-stemmed birch (*Betula utilis* var. *jacquemontii* 'Grayswood Ghost') to complement the one existing tree, a large London plane (*Platanus × hispanica*) already there on the northwest lawn. We continued to develop the planting after Lanning's death. Each spring brings a powerful swathe of purple and white crocus (*Crocus sp.*).

The curtain walling that attaches the centre block of the house to its wings screens two courtyards. We trained a creeping spindle (*Euonymus fortunei* 'Silver Queen') into both these walls' arched alcoves with great effect.

Two bronze sculptures of hounds by Mignon complete the ornamentation of the north lawn. In the early 1980s our family was staying in the British Embassy in Paris as guests of the Ambassador and his wife, Sir John and Lady Fretwell. We decided to take our children to the flea market – Marché aux Puces – at Clignancourt. We all spotted the pair of dogs at the same time but our usual ploy of ignoring anything we really wanted in the hope of negotiating a lower price was blown by the children running ahead and embracing them with shouts of 'please daddy, will you buy them?' The stallholder was apologetic. They had just been sold but not yet paid for. I left the phone number of the Embassy as our contact. The original buyer failed to materialise – the hounds were ours and arrived in England a few weeks later. Over the years, we have found the flea market to be a valuable source of garden ornaments and statuary. Several artefacts in the garden have come from there. Much later, we replaced the cistern with an eighteenth century urn made by J. M. Blashfield that Anne gave me for my sixtieth birthday. We edged the grass around it in Hornton stone cut into forty centimetre blocks eight centimetres wide by eight centimetres deep. The urn's new location stemmed from a note seeking suggestions about where to put it that I'd written to George Carter, the garden designer and historian who came to advise us in the late 1990s.

The southern lawn, half-contained by a castellated yew hedge, opens to allow a panoramic view of uninterrupted countryside. In Victorian times, this lawn was divided into flowerbeds but no sign remains of them now apart from a charming photograph *c*.1860 of

Betula utilis var. *jacquemontii* 'Grayswood Ghost'.

1765 cistern with Michael Wodhull's initials.

Red oak near the ha-ha and the tulip tree planted in 1980.

Above Euonymus fortunei 'Silver Queen'. *Right* Colour on the Main Drive from purple and white crocus.

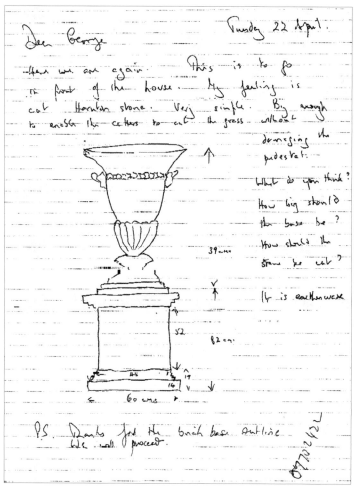

Michael's note to George Carter.

The J. M. Blashfield urn.

the beds being tended by bowler-hatted gardeners. At the west end stood the magnificent cedar of Lebanon (*Cedrus libani*) that Anne described in Chapter One falling in such a dignified way. The gap created by its demise called for the extension of the castellated yew hedge, and the new section is now approaching the scale of the original. Against the wall of the house was a Victorian summer house which we have restored.

The lawn, which we edged in steel much later, provided the perfect helicopter landing pad for a Minister of Aerospace and subsequently Defence Secretary but the depressions left behind had to be restored to make a lawn of a quality appropriate to its surroundings. A gravel path separated the lawn from two herbaceous borders that

Above Castellated yew buttresses on the South Lawn. *Right* Bronze hound by Mignon.

One of the two pairs of golden fastigiate yews (*Taxus baccata* 'Fastigiata Aureomarginata') on the Front Lawn.

Castellated yew buttresses protect borders from south-west winds.

Victorian gardeners on the South Lawn in a W. H. Dupe photo.

line the brick walls of the courtyards. Little remains except a magnificent climbing rose (*Rosa* 'Compassion'). The impressive Coalbrookdale gates mentioned in Chapter One enclose this rather private area.

The mixed border beds were too narrow for their position. Originally Lanning had advised us to widen them, plant them with shrubs and border them with a grass strip. In 2007 George Carter looked at the area again because we wanted to replace the shrubbery with two herbaceous borders. We moved the shrubs to the main drive near the stables, replaced the grass strip with brick edging and I took over the design. Recently we had to totally redesign the planting. There are many ways of saying this, but there is only one truth. The heights were wrong, the colours clashed, there were gaps and over-planting. I screwed up! In 2015 I started again.

With work in the immediate environs of the house under way, the next step was to look further into the wings of the horseshoe itself. To the west of the South Lawn, the Coalbrookdale gates lead to the Spring Garden. Lanning's help here was the selection of two most interesting limes: *Tilia kiusiana*, a large shrub with tiny leaves, and *Tilia henryana*, a medium-sized tree which has early leaves that are heavily-toothed and in a range of delicate pinks. Anne thinks it's better.

Past the Spring Garden a path leads south to our lake, inevitably called Lake Walk. Both sides are lined by snowdrops methodically relocated over many years by Frank Gurney, a local gardener who worked for us for nearly thirty years. The flowering season is now being lengthened by introducing wild daffodils (*Narcissus pseudonarcissus*) and sapphire anemone which are spreading south enthusiastically. Giant yews line either side of the path. We have interspersed them

Rosa 'Compassion' on a south-facing wall.

with a wide range of trees and shrubs, including *Callicarpa bodinieri* with its striking purple berries.

Two merit particular attention. The Burns' Day Storm in January 1990 brought down the famous 1400-year-old Selborne Yew that had been such a feature of the churchyard at St Mary's in Selborne, Hampshire. Its girth was an enormous twenty-six feet and it was taller than the church tower. Michael Mates, a friend who was MP for East Hampshire from 1974 to 2010, obtained two potted cuttings from the Alice Holt Research Station, who had advised St Mary's. In September 1993 Michael wrote to me explaining that he had no space for them. One of them flourishes today with us. Three years later Hugh Johnson, the wine writer and horticulturist, reminded us of Repton's perceptive advice to gardeners: 'The axe is my pencil.'

The garden tea house beside the Spring Garden gates.

The Coalbrookdale gates open into the Spring Garden.

The charming path alongside Lanning's Walk.

Snowdrops on Lake Walk, planted with dedication by Frank Gurney.

Above The mass of anemones turn Lake Walk to a sea of blue. *Right* Startling berries of *Callicarpa bodinieri*.

THE SELBORNE YEW
AND TRUMPETER'S GRAVE.

The Selborne Yew lives on in our cuttings.

The second tree to draw a specialist's eye is our lime (*Tilia endo-chrysea*). In 2005 I spoke at a conference and was rewarded with a small specimen. The original was collected in Guangdong in 1993 by Dr Donald Pigott and his wife Sheila, who is also a biologist. I first met Donald when he was Director of the Cambridge University Botanic Garden. Ours is a scion grafted on to *Tilia platyphyllos* rootstock by Brian Humphrey, ex-Hillier and Notcutts nurseries, who propagates and grows rare and unusual plants. This tree is rare in cultivation and to our great satisfaction it flowered for the first time in 2015.

On the house's eastern side, a path leads to the Walled Garden across a stone and iron bridge spanning Marston Brook. You pass the Rose Garden to the right and then walk past the Summer House and tennis court. On your left there is an L-shaped shrubbery following the fence line of the northern field. Although it has become known as Lanning's Walk, the title is something of a misnomer because, although Lanning Roper began the work and indeed indicated much

of its early planting, very little of his design remains. You approach the walk through a gap in a yew hedge framed by two fastigiate horn-beams (*Carpinus betulus* 'Fastigiata') that came from the Liverpool Garden Festival (see Chapter Seven). Meandering through ornamental trees that we began to plant in the early 1980s, after 175 paces the path turns ninety degrees left into a vista that's also 175 paces long. It directs your eyes up to the entrance to the Sculpture Garden (described in detail in Chapter Seven). Originally the vista was only half that long. Richard Carew Pole, a friend and onetime president of the Royal Horticultural Society, looked at it and was blunt. 'You can't have a vista that short,' he said. 'You must double it.' He was quite right. We did.

We had originally agreed to Lanning's proposed shelterbelt – larch (*Laryx sp.*), horse chestnut, turkey oak (*Quercus cerris*) and syc-amore – along the border with the North Park but later replaced it. We had embarked on our plans to build an arboretum – I'll explain

Tilia endochrysea in flower in late summer 2015.

why shortly – and we needed the space. The trees we'd planted had grown energetically and it was interesting to see which emerged as the winner. By a short head the turkey oak topped the others.

When we arrived at Thenford there were rubbish dumps close to the house. Old bottles, rusted pots, pans and the detritus of yesteryear dating back a century or more. Here was the world of today's car boot sale but that world was yet to come, so it all found its way to the rubbish dump, apart from a small bottle collection made by one of the villagers. We cleared virtually everything apart from a giant oak, a line of yews and a few remaining limes. We also widened the area at the expense of the North Park. Architect John Taylor introduced us to Simon Winter from North Wales. We commissioned him to sculpt a limestone swan inspired by the image on my signet ring.

Spring bulbs, herbaceous ground cover, shrubs and trees now border the long L-shaped walk. There are many fine things here. My mother and sister gave us two western yellow pines (*Pinus pon-*

Swan sculpture inspired by Michael's signet ring.

Northern leg of Lanning's Walk.

Lanning's Walk cleared early in the 1980s.

derosa) and a blue cedar of Lebanon (*Cedrus libani* 'Glauca') in 1982. The spruce (*Picea likiangensis*) and the purple version of the fastigiated beech from Dawyck (*Fagus sylvatica* 'Dawyck Purple') – along with a poplar (*Populus balsamifera*) and a range of *Acers*, *Prunus*, magnolias and conifer– create a powerful spring show. The *Magnolia × proctoriana* does particularly well here too and the pagoda dogwood (*Cornus alternifolia*) is another success.

We remember Lanning Roper with great affection. It is a source of constant amusement to reflect upon our clash of character. I am the first to acknowledge that I wanted to rush on and get things done. Lanning spent a lot of time explaining to me, and then often trying to persuade Anne to persuade me, that gardening is a long-term business. You have to take your time. The letters he wrote are full of this advice. He would have endorsed the mistakes acknowledged in this book with a loud 'I told you so'. The truth lies somewhere in the middle. I should have listened more but not so much that the projects'

Blue Atlas cedar planted in 1982.

Cornus alternifolia also in Lanning's Walk.

Populus balsamifera.

progress was too slow. Lanning's death left a void. It was a year or so before we could bring ourselves to choose another designer.

This book lets us come clean about our lack of knowledge and experience. Things could have turned out a great deal worse without the help and advice of Lanning and so many others who followed. We can only describe a few of those to whom we are greatly indebted and I am going to start with Harold Hillier. At the time of our move to Thenford, I held the environment portfolio in the Shadow Cabinet. I was responsible for the Conservative Party's mobilisation of our local government supporters. We were advancing on all fronts and in 1976 swept to victory in the local authority elections. I was assisted by a friend, Charlie Shelburne (now Lord Lansdowne), who owned a magnificent home and arboretum, Bowood, in Wiltshire. It was our introduction to Harold Hillier (and his then curator Roy Lancaster) by Charlie at our moment of greatest uncertainty and, soon after, to John Ropner who owned Thorp Perrow Arboretum in Yorkshire, which played such a decisive part in guiding our direction at Thenford.

The Hillier family have been nurserymen since 1864. With the demise of the Veitch Nurseries in 1914, Hillier became the pre-eminent British nursery. Harold headed the firm – which had been started by his grandfather Edwin in 1864 – after his father Edwin Lawrence died in 1944. In 1953 Harold planted an arboretum alongside the family's commercial nursery near Romsey in Hampshire. It now houses one of the largest collections of hardy (woody) plants in the contemporary world. He gave it to Hampshire County Council in 1977. The Queen Mother opened it on their behalf in 1978. It was renamed Sir Harold Hillier Gardens.

Harold has been described as the walking dictionary of the plant world. He travelled extensively, often with groups from the International Dendrology Society, acquiring seeds or appropriate material to add to his nursery's offering. He is particularly reputed to have introduced an oak (*Quercus rysophylla*) from Mexico to the UK – an initiative described as one of the best introductions of the past half-century. He is also associated with the *Magnolia macrophylla* subsp. *dealbata*. He was a forerunner of the conservation movement and was happy to point out to journalists: 'Others talk about it; I do it.' Beyond question, Harold was one of the world's outstanding horticulturists of his generation.

Anne and I first met Harold at the Hillier Gardens in 1978. It was a formative moment in the development of our plans for Thenford: it inspired us to create an arboretum. By this time, it had become increasingly likely that the Conservatives would win the forthcoming election. A ministerial post would leave little time to replant the run-down woodlands. We explained our dilemma to Harold. We had no idea of what would grow at Thenford or what to plant where. We asked him to guide us. He took immense trouble and paid us several visits before preparing a list proposing a large collection of trees and shrubs that he thought would prosper in our conditions.

We accepted his suggestions and in 1978 and 1979 huge quantities of plants arrived. Lanning began the process of choosing sites for the plants although Harold also drew designs on large scale maps we printed up from the local Ordnance Survey maps. It was working with the two of them and visiting other collections that spurred on the idea of collecting as we rebuilt the dilapidated woods.

Of course, the plants from Hillier were all labelled and many were in pots but despite Harold's guidance there was no way we could plant out such quantities in their designated positions. We decided to line them out in the Walled Garden. Two mistakes. First, the labels became a target for birds, particularly tits and, over time, we were left with quite a few unidentified plants. The second error was even more shaming: one of the gardeners actually lined out the plants without removing the pots. This was not immediately visible. It wasn't until things began to go wrong in dry weather that the cause of the problem was unearthed. Fortunately, the damage was limited.

Unwittingly, Harold also played a central role in my political learning curve in understanding the dark arts of Sir Humphrey, the

The entrance to Lanning's Walk, coming from the house.

Twenty-acre pasture south of our house.

senior civil servant as portrayed in the famous television series *Yes Minister*. Each Secretary of State is invited every six months to nominate two candidates for knighthoods and a range of other honours. I believed Harold had made an outstanding and very personal contribution to our wider environment as a horticulturist and small businessman. My officials at the Department of the Environment resisted my instruction that he be my first preference. Their first and wholly legitimate argument was that his preferment was much more a matter for the Ministry of Agriculture, Fisheries and Food. Peter Walker, its Minister, explained to me that he would support any proposal of mine but he could not elevate a horticulturist above more pressing claims from agriculture. Harold's name went in on top of my list.

When the subsequent Honours List was published, I was angered to discover that it contained no reference to the new Sir Harold. Mr Hillier had disappeared as my list journeyed upwards for Prime Ministerial approval. This happened another three times until, exasperated, I took the matter to Margaret Thatcher herself. She was, of course, completely unaware of what had transpired. Mr Harold was elevated to Sir Harold in the New Year's Honours List on Friday, 31 December 1982. I was moved to the Ministry of Defence in 1983. It would have been difficult to achieve a similar result there. Sir Harold died, aged eighty, in 1985.

A motorway construction site.

The view from the house to the lake's eastern end.

There was another happy consequence of that first visit we made to the Hillier Nursery in 1978. Besides Harold, we met Roy Lancaster. Roy was the first Curator of the Sir Harold Hillier Gardens and had helped Harold catalogue Charlie Shelburne's collection. Possessed of a proverbial knowledge of plants, he had travelled widely across the world in his search for new material and accumulated considerable experience of the growing conditions of plants in their natural state. His book *Plantsman's Paradise – Travels in China* is an epic of its sort and an inspiration for anyone interested in understanding the origins of so many of our favourite plants.

We were thrilled when, in 1984, Roy accepted our invitation to come to Thenford. We had at last found an advisor to fill the gap Lanning had left. Roy's recommendations included 'advice on the maintenance and future development of those areas already planted' with the ominous follow-on: 'Certainly advice is urgently needed on the thinning and relocation of trees planted too closely.'

Reading back over Roy's letters, his knowledge, enthusiasm and helpfulness speak volumes about the man. They are full of detail and description of his recommended plants. With their names carefully underlined, his observations would follow, often including details of where he personally had seen them in the wild and where, if possible, they could be obtained. His letters are themselves a collector's guide to botanic nurseries, seed collectors, and propagators. His language reveals not just the knowledge but the passion and enthusiasm that characterises his commitment to horticulture.

I had asked him about the problem of marginal water planting. His letter contains advice he had obtained from John Bond, who was in charge of the gardens in Windsor Great Park, and Tony Schilling, former curator of Wakehurst Place and honorary president of The Tree Register, rejecting the use of boarding as an edge. But Roy's own advice was simple. The point to bear in mind when deciding whether to board or not is that the steeper the bank the more difficult it is to establish plants. Lessen the incline and the more likely you are to succeed. Straight to the point and well worth remembering. I noticed that in his letter of December 1989 Roy had just begun to help Sir Nicholas Bacon with his collection. Nico became president of the Royal Horticultural Society in 2013.

Roy wrote to us in April 1985: 'I am as excited as you about the plans for revamping the wildfowl enclosures with their ponds.' He urged particularly that using waterside perennials would bring on extra dimensions and, in warning against 'bittiness', reiterated earlier advice to plant boldly and think of the whole length in terms of a Himalayan valley or Asiatic glade. He followed with a long list of suitable perennials. He had already suggested we plant shrubs for autumn colour in groups of three to six.

Roy had a profound knowledge of the plants in our collection and was invaluable in placing them widely within the arboretum. I will describe later how, in 1986, the present arrangement of 'Chinatown' was achieved during one of his visits.

Years later, in July 2011, it was from Roy that we first received a copy of *Champion Trees of Britain & Ireland* by Owen Johnson, which had been recently published by the Royal Botanic Gardens, Kew. We had entertained colleagues from The Tree Register in the summer of 2011; the book was a thank you present. There are forty-six Thenford trees listed as County or National Champions. Owen had taken over from Alan Mitchell who, with Victoria Hallett, was running the National Tree Register in 1986 after leaving the Forestry Commission. They visited Thenford on the recommendation of Jim Russell and listed twenty-one of our mature trees as worthy of note.

I was especially pleased to write in support of recognition for Roy in 2007 and disappointed that we were not successful. But in 2014 Roy was appointed CBE in the Queen's Birthday Honours. This was the second well-deserved recognition that owes its origins to the Sir Harold Hillier Gardens.

While our introduction to Harold and Roy were most significant steps, two other Hillier employees have played significant parts in creating Thenford: Keith Rushforth and Allen Coombes, to whom we are also very grateful. Keith took over from Roy as the Sir Harold Hillier Gardens Curator in 1980. He was and is an intrepid plant hunter. His book *Conifers* clearly reveals his expertise. Everyone who collects seeds is very familiar with the trauma of failure. They will be familiar with the rows of empty pots where germination failed. Success, on the other hand, has its challenges. Germination of a dozen – perhaps dozens – of tiny trees or shrubs could persuade you to choose a handful and throw the rest away. But one feels a responsibility, having brought them into this world. That's the way it works. Homes have to be found. I was lucky in August 1987 when Keith phoned to say he was having a cull. To this day I can see the rows of pots, each with a conifer seedling, in the Walled Garden. That was the foundation of our conifer collection and included a Burmese spruce (*Picea farreri*).

What made our memory of that day indelible was Keith telling us that, because he and his wife Heather were moving, there were a couple of rare wild-collected trees about six feet high in the garden that we could have. To move such trees in mid-August needs more than skill. Luck was with us. Today the oak (*Quercus semecarpifolia*) must be one of the best of its sort in the country, the fir (*Abies vejarii*) is over sixty feet high and both are listed in *Champion Trees of Britain & Ireland*.

Keith has provided us with many species over the years – about 1600. A lot have been the results of seed-hunting expeditions which we have helped to finance. It was a particular pleasure when Keith rang to say that in celebration of our friendship and support he had given the name *Sorbus heseltinei* to a new plant he had found in Xizang, Tibet. We arranged for Gillian Barlow to paint a picture of it and were delighted to see the picture and Keith's monograph *A preliminary revision of the Sino-Himalayan whitebeams* in the *International Dendrology Society's Yearbook 2009*, published July 2010.

John Ropner, another of Charlie Shelburne's introductions, had inherited the arboretum at Thorp Perrow, near Bedale, North

Looking from the house towards the lake's western end.

Yorkshire, when his father Leonard died in 1977. Sir Leonard, MP for Sedgefield in the 1920s, had started planting an arboretum in the grounds of Thorp Perrow Hall in 1931. Sadly, the ravages of time took their toll. Minimal maintenance over many decades meant that John was faced with the daunting challenge of bringing the collection back to its intended standard. For us, when we visited Thorp Perrow in the late 1970s, it was a warning about what happens if the necessary care is not forthcoming. But even in the arboretum's disarray, it was possible to see the exciting range, rarity and quality of what was left of Leonard's vision. Walking round the eighty-five-acre arboretum more than thirty years after our first visit, it is immensely exciting to see how Sir John and his third wife Niki not only restored but significantly enhanced Thorp Perrow so that it is now one of the country's better collections. Sadly, John died as we were completing this book.

John took us to another impressive collection in the grounds of Castle Howard. It was under the direction of the distinguished plantsman Jim Russell. His reclamation of Ray Wood and the neighbouring planting live up to the attraction of Castle Howard's magnificent architecture. Looking back, it is all too easy to see how these visits fired our ambition. But visits can be frustrating. Six or seven years later I squeezed a second visit to Castle Howard into a ministerial tour. The growth was as exciting as Jim's generosity. He had frames full of small plants. I had to keep an eye on my watch as the ministerial visit threatened to cut short my ability to load up the gifts.

At the invitation of friends, we made other, coincidental visits. The gardens of the United Kingdom are an asset of irreplaceable and immeasurable value. There is no better way to visualise and plan your own garden than to look at the work of others and to see how

they have exploited opportunities or overcome problems. There is, of course, a tension about doing that. Very rapidly you become so engrossed in what you're doing at home that you resent time away. We should have done more of it.

One garden that certainly made an indelible impression on us was Hidcote Manor Garden near Chipping Campden, towards the west of the Cotswolds. Created by Lawrence Johnston in the early twentieth century, it combines sharply contrasting vistas and designs in a series of interconnecting rooms. The mood and pace changes dramatically as clever screening and well-constructed hedges provide backgrounds to quite different but interlinked gardens in an area no bigger than ten-and-a-half acres. No visit to Hidcote should miss out its neighbour Kiftsgate, where the rose of that name originated. Kiftsgate Court Gardens present you with a wide range of immaculately maintained and clearly labelled rare and choice plants in a relatively compact setting. Open terraces, a dramatic yew garden with an imposing water feature and a precipitous cliff create stirring contrasts. The roses are displayed with military-like discipline. Apart from the famous rambler *Rosa filipes* 'Kiftsgate', which Peter Beale described as 'the most vigorous of all', other favourites of ours include the ramblers *Rosa* 'Rambling Rector', 'Bobbie James', 'Seagull', 'Paul's Himalayan Musk' and 'The Garland'. They are a spectacular sight in early summer.

Westonbirt, created by Robert Steyner Holford in 1829, is on a different scale. We saw it first in the autumn of the year when its thirty-year expansion was just beginning. Over the years we have been drawn back each October to revel in the glory of the Japanese maples (*Acer palmatum* cvs.) in their autumn colour. Sheltering under the canopy of the giant plantings of the eighteenth century, these maples

Looking north towards the house – an inspiring view in all weathers.

Guy Taplin cormorants.

enjoy the light shade and are a breathtaking attraction. Try visiting on the twenty-third of October, which seems to work for us and happens to be Anne's birthday. We received much encouragement and help from Les Pearce, a vice president of the Friends of Westonbirt Arboretum, in our early decisions. The most adventurous was a loan of a tree lopper. Its elevated arm could get you and its electric saw up into branches fifteen to twenty feet above ground and, hair-raising though it was, you could actually drive the machine from the elevated platform. This was long before the days of health and safety legislation.

While the decisions we took in the early years were, unsurprisingly, centred on the areas close to the house, there was one exception: a lake. Just before we exchanged contracts in 1976, we had been shattered when we were told that Jean Summers wished to keep the twenty-five-acre woodland and bathing lake near Thenford Lodge. We understood: it had been her life and she wanted it undisturbed, but we were very disappointed. We'd secured the option to acquire the lake and woodland later but in the meantime Jean's decision left us with no lake. A solution presented itself: in the twenty-acre pasture to the south of our house a tiny, boggy stream left Jean's lake and crossed to the other side. Cattle had been stuck in it frequently so it was fenced with ugly barbed wire to deter them. It needed no imagination to see that a dam was all that was necessary to create not only our own new lake but also a wonderful view from the house.

When we started to dig, we found we were lucky with the composition of the soil. Six foot down we struck blue Oxfordshire Clay – the perfect base. For a few weeks it looked like a motorway construction site as large quantities of soil were consolidated into a formidable dam and two islands. Day one brought a trickle as the diverted stream was allowed to flow again; three months later we had a three-acre lake. But we should have decided what to plant on the islands long before we flooded the lake. Wheelbarrows or dumpers could have conveyed the plants easily, sparing the gardeners many trips in wobbly rowing boats. Mistake!

Chapter Four

THE MAIN DRIVE, TOP DRIVE & MARSTON ROAD

A place through which to wander and soak up the atmosphere beneath the ever-growing

canopy – a place where the impact of autumn colour is particularly satisfying.

by Anne Heseltine

THENFORD
The Creation of an
English Garden

WHEN MICHAEL WODHULL BUILT the manor house at Thenford the drive led through a mile-long, tree-lined avenue from the main Banbury-Brackley road. The entrance way and any gates have long since disappeared, although we have replanted the avenue with oaks instead of the miscellany of species put there by later owners. However, at some stage, Wodhull decided to create a drive for his new home from a minor road leading into the village from the north. It was a surprise to us that, with such ambitions for his eighteenth century house, he was apparently uninterested in the entrance. When we arrived, the tarmac drive to the house, with its speed-limiting bumps and '*Warning – children*' signs, was much as one would expect but the gate was an ordinary five-bar farm gate set into a fence of vertical railway sleepers. We moved it to a suitably modest location but it soon disintegrated.

We decided to install new gates into a stone wall, something more in keeping with our view of what Wodhull himself would have liked. We chose Richard Quinnell's Rowhurst Forge in Leatherhead,

The 'functional' original gate.

Surrey. Their work was bold, strong and had a feeling for period. The gates they made for us were tall, simple, double-width and set into stone piers, with a pedestrian opening at the side, and an arching overhang above. Another mistake! We hadn't thought about the height of the overhang. It proved to be too low for large vans, horse boxes and lorries. All too often we saw the gate piers damaged and the iron work buckled. After the third disaster, we had to put up warning notices and finally Jim Horrobin (who, by coincidence, had once worked with Quinnell; see Chapter Eight for more about Jim) designed iron railings that emphasized the narrow entry.

The most distressing incident happened during the arrival of a painting of an aerial view of the house and arboretum that I had commissioned as a surprise present for Michael on our silver wedding anniversary. The painter was Jonathan Warrender, who had entered into the spirit of the thing and lurked behind trees if Michael was around. While he was on-site, he lived in one of the stable flats and only came up to the house for lunch if Michael was away. He had decided to deliver the painting personally and to meet Michael at last. I was very excited because I knew the painting was a success and was dying to see Michael's reaction. Its arrival wasn't quite as auspicious as I had expected. Jonathan had hired a van and driven all the way from his home in Scotland. He came up the drive slowly and responsibly, but all was not well. As he approached, we could see a decided dent in the van's roof, harbouring a small pile of Hornton stone. A very flushed and embarrassed Jonathan and wife disembarked. We felt so sorry for them; all those months of work, the exhausting drive from Scotland, and now they had destroyed our gates! Fortunately, the painting was unharmed and Jonathan's insurance company paid up. We had a very jolly lunch, and parted on good terms. But, oh how we wished we had measured the height of the gates before they'd gone up!

After choosing the design of the gates, our attention turned to the wall. We ignored the well-meaning advice of a neighbour about the railway sleepers: 'Good idea to keep those – stops the deer.' The fence only bordered the road and was therefore ineffective – it was hideous, too. We chose to build a stone wall, which would be expensive but long-lasting. It was hard to find a dry stone waller who would take on such a big project. A local firm of builders, Woottons, had a man but he would have to break off from time to time to carry out smaller jobs elsewhere. Sid Wootton, in April 1977, offered us a stonemason at £20 per yard for a two-faced stone wall or £10 per yard for a wall with stone on the outside and breeze blocks inside. For cost reasons, we decided to have Hornton stone on the outside facing the lane, with the breeze blocks on the inside. I remembered this with gloomy regrets when I was planting 2000 ivy plants (*Hedera sp.*) as a screen the following year.

In the meantime, the stonemason had started off in fine style, and we would watch admiringly while the wall gradually began to extend along the lane. But we had not foreseen that this would be one of the harshest winters of the past thirty years. We noticed that the builder seemed to attend less and less frequently, always seeming to have a vital 'small' job to complete. And who could blame him? I was struggling to get Alexandra to school locally – once, she was driven there on the farm tractor. Eventually the wall, capped with jagged stones, was complete. We were more than content with the result. Thirty-five years later, it looks as if it has been there for ever. Much to my annoyance, you can't see my much-hated ivy plants on the inside now. The laurels and yew trees planted as a wind break have done the screening job for us – and much more efficiently.

With the plans for new gates and the wall in place, we needed to continue and develop planting plans on either side of the entrance way. The drive itself turns south towards the house, dividing a grass area which was planted largely with mature sycamores. To the north, an open area bordered by the new wall on one side and a field fence on the other had no formal feature but invited the creation of an avenue of new trees.

We started to clear some of the sycamores early on. It was a huge job involving the felling of mature trees. Once the trees came down

The original gate rehung in Lake Walk.

The new gates made by Richard Quinnell.

and were cleared we had to confront the question of their roots which, if left, could for ever be a breeding ground for honey fungus. We employed stump grinders which certainly removed any visible remainder of the trees above ground but left the bulk of the root below. A more exotic solution involved using high explosives which literally blew the stump out of the ground and created a massive hole. These amateurish but stimulating activities obviously failed to impress the powers that be. A more dramatic intervention followed: the gigantic gale of 1986.

That morning, Rupert and I were having breakfast on our own in the dining room at the back of the house. Suddenly, the windows started rattling in their frames. Dust and leaves came through the gaps in the sashes. With great presence of mind, Rupert leapt to his feet and hastily fixed the wooden shutters with their iron bars. The whole house seemed to shake. The dogs started to howl. This wasn't the vicious wind that hit London a year later in October 1987, but the tail end of a cyclone that had swept across America, the Atlantic, and was running itself down across the English Midlands. It spiralled across our land, leaving some areas untouched but some devastated. We did not dare venture outside until about four that afternoon.

We were shocked by the damage. The roof of a barn adjoining one of the cattle yards had been wrenched off and hurled about 100 yards out into a ploughed field. The tops of two beautiful cedars alongside the house had been torn off and chucked on the ground as if by a petulant baby giant. Their lower branches were intact and the trees flourish today. But mayhem reigned along the main drive. Thankfully, the wonderful giant redwood (*Sequoiadendron giganteum*) had survived. It had been my landmark as I rode around the country-

Some of the damage from the storm of 1986.

Anne among the roots of a giant sycamore that was one of the casualties.

The Main Drive section of the arboretum was particularly hard hit.

side in our early days at Thenford, always looming up in the distance, so that I was never lost. But the sycamores, beeches, elders and general 'junk' had been badly hit: the gale had done a wonderfully selective job for us. We had virtually a clear site to work with but a huge amount of debris to pick up.

The drive to the house is awash with colour as spring unfolds. It would be nice to claim that clever planting lies behind the views that have developed over the years to create charming glimpses of the house as you approach. The truth is that it is the luck of the game but no less attractive for that. The early flowering cherry (*Prunus* 'Kursar') has a cypress (*Chamaecyparis lawsoniana* 'Winston Churchill') in the background. A magnificent blue Atlas cedar – *Cedrus atlantica* (Glauca Group) 'Glauca' – backs up an *Acer palmatum* 'Nomura' and a *Magnolia stellata* 'Centennial'. With the drifts of golden daffodils beneath them, the sight on that first warm day in March lifts the soul and straightens the back. Bluebells are re-establishing under the American lime *Tilia americana*.

Some of our earliest plantings were on the main drive. The two different tulip trees came from Esveld in Holland: one of them – *Liriodendron tulipifera* 'Aureomarginatum' – is heavily variegated with golden markings and the other – *Liriodendron tulipifera* 'Mediopictum' – has green leaves with a prominent yellow patch in the middle. A curiosity is the chimaera + *Laburnocytisus* 'Adamii'. A dendrological joke – a graft hybrid that originated in France in the early nineteenth century – it produces yellow laburnum and purple broom flowers on the same tree. There is a very attractive crab apple (*Malus florentina*) planted close to a *Sorbus* 'Chinese Lace' given to us by Alan Cochrane, Scottish Editor of *The Daily Telegraph*. A wild-collected Mexican oak (*Quercus affinis*) regularly produces acorns whilst a particularly fine pin oak (*Quercus palustris*) enthusiastically demonstrates its characteristic low-swooping branches. Mark and Gabriella Schreiber (Lord and Lady Marlesford) gave us the Caucasian elm (*Zelkova carpinifolia*) in the 1980s.

As you enter through the gates, the area to the north lacks formality and has no constructed feature. Known as the Top Drive until it bears right and becomes Marston Road, it is a place through which to wander along a cleared central path. At its eastern end the atmosphere changes again as you reach the Mount, Amelanchier Avenue and the Sculpture Garden described in Chapter Seven. The Rill (Chapter Ten) and the Trough Garden (Chapter Twelve) are close by.

Without obvious eye-stoppers or formality, interest within the Top Drive focuses on the trees themselves. The first of them, just inside the gates, is a mature beech that's probably one of the very few survivors of Wodhull's own planting. It has lived through storms and drought for over 200 years. We arrived at the time of the 1976 drought and it was tragic to see the majestic beech trees give up one by one, but this one survived. Mature yews and hollies (*Ilex aquifolium*) are dotted about, and the odd ash, hornbeam, horse chestnut and sweet chestnut (*Castanea sativa*) survive but they are the isolated exceptions.

Left Cedrus atlantica (Glauca Group) 'Glauca'. *Above* Spring time on the Main Drive.

Above The house looking south from the Top Drive. *Next page* Giant redwood dwarfs its surroundings.

Early flowering *Prunus* 'kursar'.

Bluebells under the American lime.

The +*Laburnocytisus* 'Adamii' – where laburnam and broom flowers bloom on the same tree.

Above Flowering cherries in the Top Drive. *Right Prunus* 'Matsumae-fuki'.

Prunus 'Matsumae-yaekotobuki'.

We have avoided grouping genera in specific areas but among some 400 plantings in this area, fifty are different rowans (*Sorbus spp.*) including our common red-berried *Sorbus aucuparia* and two different forms of it, the yellow-berried *Sorbus aucuparia* var. *xanthocarpa* and *Sorbus* 'Hilling's Spire'. Hugh McAllister, the resident botanist at Liverpool University gardens at Ness in 1980, gave us the rowans *Sorbus devoniensis* – collected by Keith Rushforth – and *Sorbus caloneura*, which is vulnerable to late frost but thankfully has always recovered. Pride of place is given to *Sorbus heseltinei*, mentioned in Chapter Three, which Keith found in the Himalayas. Elizabeth Banks, then President of the Royal Horticultural Society, conducted the formal naming at a dinner we gave at Thenford for The Garden Society in 2011. There are a number of oaks in this area, including *Quercus rysophylla*, which John Grimshaw regards as one of the best introductions of the post-war period.

John is Director of the Castle Howard Arboretum Trust in Yorkshire and was formerly Gardens Manager at Colesbourne Park, near Cheltenham in Gloucestershire. He has a formidable academic record and years of practical experience in estate management. In 2009, with

Above The John Major pumpkin ash. *Right Sorbus heseltinei.*

Fagus sylvatica 'Purpurea Tricolor'.

Sorbus heseltinei

Ross Bayton, he completed *New Trees: Recent Introductions to Cultivation* which was published by the Royal Botanic Gardens, Kew, on behalf of the International Dendrology Society. While at Colesbourne Park he had co-authored *Snowdrops* with Matt Bishop and Aaron Davis.

In one respect the *Quercus rysophylla* – or rather, where we planted it – qualifies as a mistake: trees either side of it – the poplar (*Populus alba* 'Richardii') and *Malus prattii* – will have to go to allow it growing space. Other oaks in this area include *Quercus robur* Cristata Group and Fastigiata Group, *rubra* 'Bolte's Gold', and *kelloggii*, *cerris*, *ellipsoidalis*, *ithaburensis* subsp. *macrolepis* and *macranthera*. Beneath the growing canopy of large trees, magnolias thrive happily. So do forms of *Acer palmatum*. When John Bond was in charge of the Savill Garden at Windsor he gave us a collection of the magnolia hybrids known as 'the girls', named after the ladies in his office – 'Daphne', 'Judy', 'Randy' and 'Susan'. 'Judy's' colour is very dramatic and one cannot miss a trio of 'Randy'. We have balanced the harsher colours with their yellow cousins.

The ever-growing canopy includes two forms of native beech, one of which has purple leaves (*Fagus sylvatica* Atropurpurea Group) and another which has purple leaves tinged with a pink edging (*Fagus sylvatica* 'Purpurea Tricolor'). We must also mention the pumpkin ash (*Fraxinus profunda*) planted to commemorate John and Norma Major's visit to us after Michael's heart attack in 1993. Finally, magnificent hollies we inherited provide ideal homes for clematis (*Clematis spp.*) and roses, including several from the Mattock collection referred to in Chapter Thirteen.

Quite understandably, most visitors head for the more formal parts of our garden once they have found the tearoom and associated facilities. But for those interested in the rarer plants, this walk through the arboretum is a good place to start. With a wide mixture of deciduous and evergreen trees and shrubs interspaced with conifers, you are drawn to closer examination. Curiously, this very English garden is composed of myriad imports from across the world. But it was ever so: we have followed in the steps of the Tradescants and other great plant hunters. On the edge of the Main Drive and Marston Road, the growing impact of the autumn colour is particularly satisfying and can only improve as the trees grow bigger.

Sorbus folgneri berries.

Quercus rysophylla.

Magnolia 'Randy'.

Magnolia 'Randy'.

Magnolia 'Banana Split'.

Magnolia 'Randy'.

Magnolia 'Heaven Scent'.

Magnolia × 'Loebneri'.

Magnolia 'Dark Shadow'.

Magnolia 'Anne Rosse'.

Magnolia 'Limelight'.

Magnolia 'Judy'.

Magnolia 'Judy'.

Magnolia × *soulangeana* 'Sundew'.

Autumn colour on the Main Drive...

...and autumn colour on Marston Road.

Chapter Five

THE WATER GARDENS

Water is the making of the garden: your own nature reserve, a personal therapy, every note in harmony with its background, a mirror for the things you've planted.

by Michael Heseltine

THENFORD
The Creation of an
English Garden

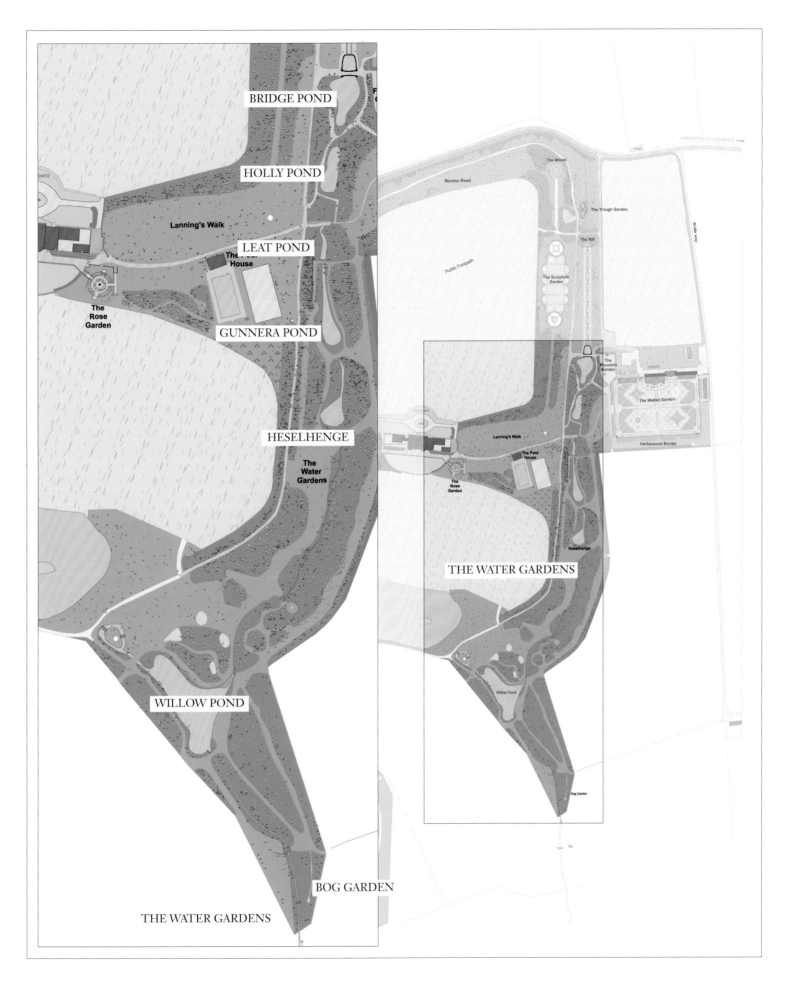

BRIDGE POND

HOLLY POND

Lanning's Walk

LEAT POND

The Pool House

The Rose Garden

GUNNERA POND

HESELHENGE

The Water Gardens

THE WATER GARDENS

WILLOW POND

BOG GARDEN

THE WATER GARDENS

THE MARSTON BROOK runs down the eastern leg of our 'horse-shoe'. It enters the arboretum through a pipe under the wall (described in detail in Chapter Ten) then flows south for about half a mile. The land around it slopes gently but for much of the way the stream is either in a deep ditch or at the bottom of a small valley bordered by farmland. Only as you approach the lower end does the land flatten into a wide, open space. Our predecessors had used this area as a holding place for a family shoot. The old pens, long unused, were visible beneath the debris. The place was abandoned although the cess pit for the house was still in use. At its lower reach, Marston Brook is joined by our other stream, which comes from the west through the fishponds, the original lake, Jean's Wood and the new lake we built in the late 1970s. United, they then flow through boggy ground to become a tributary of the River Cherwell and then the River Thames.

Through the summer, Marston Brook is just a trickle fed by the many springs close to its course. From September to May there is usually a gentle, clear six inches of water but, when it has to, it copes with winter rain of torrential proportions. The stream cuts off the Walled Garden from our house; two stone-built eighteenth century bridges provide access. Towards the northern end, a simple local authority bridge carried a public right of way. Our first plan in the late 1970s was to create an aviary by fencing in about two acres of this area using the west wall of the Walled Garden on the east side and a six-foot fox-proof fence that had much of the visual characteristics of a prisoner of war camp. We dammed the stream in five places to create five ponds and used earth-moving equipment to smooth out the sloping sides to improve access. We knew that homes would have to be found for the growing collection of plants lined out in the Walled Garden. To provide planting sites, we created as many pathways as possible though this area including, in the case of three of the ponds, at water level with oak-lined edging.

The aviary carved out a significant part of the centre of the area, leaving the top little-changed except for plantings to the west and east where an existing path and a headland formed definable edges. It was not until about twenty-five years later when we built the Rill (see Chapter Ten) that there was significant change. Below the old aviary area, the bank gradually smooths and flattens into the Statue Garden.

At the southern end of the Statue Garden, damp shady ground with a canopy of Scots pines (*Pinus sylvestris*) was extended in 1986 by the addition of the grand fir (*Abies grandis*) and the dawn redwood (*Metasequoia glyptostroboides*). They came as six-foot-tall plants that we carried from their trailer across the stream to their new home. Thirty years later they are sixty feet tall.

The walk south down through the Water Gardens finishes at the Willow Pond. The open glade is blocked off by a shrubbery behind which there is a muddy shallow kept damp by Marston Brook and our second stream. We had decided to tackle this boggy area in 1988 by creating a willow pond and a willow collection alongside it, which we called Anne's Wood. To help visitors avoid the muddy conditions around the Willow Pond we built a raised walkway of oak planks. At a

Robert Adams's restored bridge.

Reducing the slope.

Waterside paths at Gunnera Pond.

Opposite page Thirty-year old *Metasequoia glyptostroboides*.

cost of £5000 it was an expensive mistake – the many willows drained the area, which is now solid underfoot. In 1999 we removed it.

By the time we had been at Thenford for just over twenty years we had undertaken a comprehensive reclamation of this part of the garden. The structure as it is today had largely been put in place, there had been extensive planting and – one would have thought – it would be possible to concentrate on maintenance. That was not to be. Over the next ten years we systematically revisited what we had done – adding, changing and improving as we went. We decided to create a new vista from the old orchard down the eastern side of the Water Gardens. The ponds themselves needed improvement too. We also wanted to create a woodland garden lower down and, although the wet ground of the willow wood was now much drier, a boggy area remained below it which we decided to plant as a bog garden.

If I have rushed through our journey over these thirty-five years, let me now retrace our steps at a more measured pace. In theory, the collection of swans, geese, ducks and pheasants included in the aviary in the 1970s was enough to satisfy the most enthusiastic aviculturist. In practice it was a disaster. The fault was ours. Most of the week we lived in London and, not infrequently, work demanded our absence at the weekend too. Coupled with a very amateur knowledge, virtually no experience and no-one to do anything other than provide food, the disenchantment was inevitable.

Apart from the webbed feet trooping along the streamside destroying any struggling vegetation, many of the inhabitants appeared to have a personal dislike for each other, and people. One brown-eared pheasant would lie in wait and attack us by leaping into the air and using its vicious spurs to draw blood on our legs. We were only safe when we wore substantial gumboots even in the hottest weather. But we persevered and even bought a rather sophisticated German incubator to hatch pheasant eggs. In the end a succession of pheasant chicks with deformed legs put paid to that. It was too slow a learning curve. We were still persevering after my resignation as Secretary of State for Defence in 1986. My friend and fellow MP, Michael Mates, gave us a nesting box with the label 'Thenford-les-Deux-Églises' to demonstrate my determination not to abandon my political career. For those unfamiliar with the reference, it alludes to Charles de Gaulle. After his resignation as President of France's Provisional Government in 1946 he returned to his home at Colombey-les-Deux-Églises to await, as he believed, his recall to duty.

Nothing more reveals the utilitarian nature of the aviary we built than the way we named the five ponds from Marston Brook – Ponds A, B, C, D and E! The writing of this book has precipitated a revision more in keeping with their new status. Going from north to south, they are now Bridge, Holly, Leat, Gunnera and Heselhenge.

The old, north, stone bridge at the top of Bridge Pond would have served the Walled Garden, in addition to the more ornamental bridge through the orchard. The giant sweet chestnuts and a century-old English oak dominate the planting at the top of the Water Gardens.

Willow Pond on a winter's day.

Two paths encircling Bridge Pond lead to Holly Pond, which takes its name from several hollies dating back a century or more and a now-significant holly collection bought from Hillier in 1978. For all too brief a summer moment, the giant sixty-foot hollies to the east of this pond are home to *Rosa brunonii* and *Rosa henryi* which literally take over the host tree. These Asian species need careful planting. They are thugs of the plant world and show no mercy. The photograph overleaf shows their vigour.

The waterside path past Holly Pond leads to a stone arch we bought by the roadside on one of our journeys to the south of France. *Brocante* signs in France are magnets we cannot resist. Whether it's the scale and variety of the flea market at Clignancourt, the little shops at L'Isle-sur-la-Sorgue in Provence or the road-side accumulations of yesteryear, we just can't resist. We make no apologies. All over our garden are the purchases that have followed that screech of brakes on hot tarmac as another alluring sign signals *Brocante*. It is, of course, *caveat emptor*. You are on your own and must rely on your judgement. We guess our arch is late nineteenth

The gunnera fountain at Bridge Pond.

Bridge Pond unplanted.

Looking at the Rill from Bridge Pond.

Rosa brunonii and *Rosa Henryi*.

century and just the thing to balance its counterpart further downstream. In our experience, all the French roadside enterprises are well-versed in shipping purchases across the Channel and while, self-evidently, they're usually glorified junk, as garden features they are invaluable.

Holly Pond is dammed above the old bridge. When the stream flowed in its original deep cutting, it was far enough from the roots of a mature yew. Heavy machinery and substantial slabs of stone quarried from old workings on our land in 2009 created a shady, steep-sided rockery through which the water flowed under the bridge into Leat Pond. Realistically, Leat Pond isn't a pond at all – merely a slip of water a bit more than three feet wide and 100 feet long between sloping banks, with the orchard to the east and rhododendron walk to the west. We had left an old ash stump cut off at about three feet to form the base for a substantial clay pot. The pot first lived on the other side of the bridge on an old oak stump but decay had demanded a new home. A tightly-clipped holly, shaped into a ball, completed the feature.

Above Leat Pond cleared. *Below* Leat Pond now.

Arch spotted in a roadside junkyard.

Right Holly Pond. *Next page* Cascades from Holly to Leat Pond.

There are two approaches to Leat Pond. From the west, the best way is through another of our roadside acquisitions, a very early stone arch possibly dating from the eleventh or twelfth centuries. We found it one evening in an up-market antiques shop housed in an old church in Tournus, Burgundy, where we had forward-booked dinner in a Michelin-starred restaurant. We returned next morning to be quoted a price of €2000. It was too good to be true. The purchase was agreed. Delivery instructions were placed. A couple of days later the inevitable phone call explained about the missing zero. We have no regrets. The arch provides a dramatic entranceway and a splendid view. As with so many purchases of this sort, life is never as simple as it seems. Our builder, Chris McDaniel, pointed out the health and safety risk involved with this reconstructed, free-standing arch. Mention of a duty of care for visitors walking under it necessitated the addition of a framework of two powerful RSJs sunk into concrete blocks, all mercifully now hidden by yew topiary.

Darren Webster plants the holly topiary.

Above The arch from Tournus in pieces. *Right* The arch assembled.

There was another approach to Leat Pond from the old orchard to the east. In 2000 we realised that this small, inconsequential path could be widened and cleared to open up a vista stretching virtually all the way down this side of the arboretum behind Gunnera Pond, Heselhenge, the area known as Chinatown and the Statue Garden. Several mature birch remain in the border hedge, which prompted the self-selecting name Birchway.

The opening up of Birchway, past a trio of *Magnolia* 'Star Wars', provided a much wider access to Leat Pond and the opportunity to plant a range of plants in mixed borders. A significant part of our snowdrop collection is now here, as is the box (*Buxus sempervirens*) I obtained permission from Mrs Thatcher to remove from Chequers as a cutting in 1985.

Travelling south from Leat Pond, there are four different ways to go. The opening along Birchway; the two original paths to the western side which we originally cleared in the early 1980s; or in the middle along a water-level, oak-edged, bark-filled pathway down the east side of Gunnera Pond. We created this path as part of the original aviary when it was approached by a range of wooden steps but time

Birchway being prepared.

Left Birchway from the orchard. *Above* Birchway opened up.

had brought significant deterioration and in 2010 we replaced them with a ramp, a widened path and graded bank for ease of planting. We built a small rockery at the southeast corner to stabilise the bank undermined by springs feeding the pond. We had originally planted two golden weeping willows (*Salix* × *sepulcralis* var. *chrysocoma*) which, of course, grow almost before your eyes. One was moved with heavy equipment and today flourishes down near the Willow Pond. Of particular interest is the purple toothwort (*Lathraea clandestina*) given to us by Roy Lancaster that, as a parasite, lives off its roots.

Gunnera Pond, named after the *Gunnera manicata* at its southern end, begins with a narrow neck then fills out to an open space where there are two significant trees: a thirty-five-year-old *Quercus robur* 'Salicifolia' on the east bank and a further golden weeping willow the same age on the west. The dramatic foliage of the *Gunnera manicata* was also the inspiration for the fountain in Bridge Pond.

The stream then falls significantly to the next pond – Heselhenge. One of our earliest head gardeners, Alan Jones, created a waterfall there that carries his name. Above the fall there's an unusual weeping pendulus katsura (*Cercidiphyllum japonicum* f. *pendulum*) planted in 1979, and in the space between the two ponds are the three paperbark maples (*Acer griseum*) that Charlie Price, US Ambassador to the UK from 1983–89, gave us in 1986. Heselhenge derived its name from an event in the 1990s when Robert Adams, who was helping us create the Sculpture Garden, designed the placing near the pond of five large slabs of stone extracted from our land. One could not help thinking of the countless humans who built Stonehenge as we watched the sort of equipment available to us working on our modest replica.

From Heselhenge, the land divides into the Statue Garden; a flat shrubbery bordering the South Park on the west with open grass at

Left The narrow neck of Gunnera Pond. *Above* The remaining *Salix* × *sepulcralis* var. *chrysocoma*.

Previous page Gunnera and *primula* thrive in the damp ground. *Above* The south end of Gunnera Pond.

Robert Adams creating Heselhenge.

Heselhenge and the vibrant colours of its surrounding maples.

its centre; and Chinatown, a gentle slope up to Birchway on the east. One of the first trees you meet as you walk down the centre of the Statue Garden is the *Juglans mandshurica* which bears the name of Chinese Vice Premier Li Lanqing who came to lunch at Thenford in 1996. It has to be admitted that Li Lanqing didn't actually plant the tree. Indeed, if truth be told he is unlikely to know of its existence but so few people have had the opportunity to entertain such an eminent Chinese leader in their own home that the event merits appropriate recognition.

Further down, two handkerchief trees (*Davidia involucrata* and *Davidia involucrata* var. *vilmoriniana*), dominate the central area – or will, ultimately. Incidentally, the larger of the two illustrates our overplanting problem. It will not survive to its full glory as long as we spare the huge English oak behind it. The decision can be postponed but not avoided. All is not completely lost because coming up alongside the *Davidia* is another oak but this time a freak (*Quercus petraea* 'Laciniata Crispa'). The most you can say for it is that it's different and few collections have one. Very rare is the Burmese spruce I mentioned earlier. It is a species from Myanmar and Yunnan whose seeds were originally collected by plant hunter Reginald Farrer, the 'Prince of Alpine gardeners', during his 1919 expedition. Keith Rush-forth took a scion from the Farrer original under F1435 at Exbury Gardens, near Beaulieu, Hampshire, and grew our tree from a small potted plant.

Uniquely within our collection, Chinatown is reserved virtually exclusively for trees and shrubs of Chinese origin. It was laid out by Roy Lancaster over a couple of days in 1986. There have been many additions since then, including the Chinese tulip tree (*Liriodendron chinense*) and a range of species roses. We left part of the original canopy of yew, oak and ash, only clearing selectively as our new plantings matured. There is still some way to go and, of course, removing mature trees while protecting the newcomers is an expensive game of cranes and specialist tree climbers that can easily cost £1000 per tree. We have plans to make a path that creates a woodland experience.

On the west side, a modern Italian seat – appropriately weathered, doubtless by immersion in a canal – is backed by a castellated yew hedge and situated to command a view of a marble statue of Hermes that originally held aloft a torch to light up the staircase at the Brussels Opera House. Next to Hermes, a spinney of Scots pines and elders had been enlarged in 1986 by adding a dawn redwood and sweet gum (*Liquidambar styraciflua*). In 1999 we created a long, thin, curved waterside bed to the west of the stream. We revisited this area

Left Juglans mandshurica. *Above* Davidia involucrata.

with more ambitious plans in 2003. The first step included the creation of bark paths with edges formed from yew wood.

Beneath the canopy of pine, fir and dawn redwood – which provide plenty of light on the stream side to shade in the central areas – most of the planting is herbaceous or small shrubs. On the drier ground, *Epimedium epsteinii* and *E. × warleyense* are taking hold, along with foxgloves (*Digitalis spp.*) and ferns. On the damper areas, hosta cultivars, a group of umbrella plants (*Darmera peltata*), yellow skunk cabbage (*Lysichiton americanu*s) and Asian skunk cabbage (*Lysichiton camtschatcensis*), along with *Rodgersia podophylla*, Japanese flag (*Iris ensata*), primulas and the large plate-like *Astilboides tabularis*, do well. A collection of *Podophyllum*, including *P. delavayi, difforme, peltatum, versipelle, versipelle* 'Spotty Dotty' and *Sinopodophyllum hexandrum* is gaining ground. But you can't escape the *Arisaema tortuosum*. There are also several other varieties of *Arisaema* grown from seed donated by the Savill Gardens that contrast with different ferns, but the *Arisaema tortuosum* are now some three feet high and are the talking point for visitors unfamiliar with this exciting genera.

Moving on, beyond the shrubbery that defines the end of the Statue Garden, there is an interesting collection of horse chestnuts with which we were much helped by Robert Grimsey (see Chapter Thirteen). Finally, there is Willow Pond, Anne's Wood and, further

downstream, our attempts at the Bog Garden.

In the 1980s we built a dam at the lower end of the boggy ground where Marston Brook merges with the other stream. Having recontoured the land to reuse the surplus material dredged from the lake area to the west, we rapidly had a home for willows and elders. We had established contact with Dr Ing Jindřich Chmelař of Mendel University in Brno, Czechoslovakia, who had founded the Řícmanice Arboretum and oversaw a huge collection of *Salix* (willows). I had been given his name by Desmond Meikle who himself had a collection of willows. I wrote to Dr Ing Chmelař in September 1988 and sent a list of our existing collection. We were able to visit Czechoslovakia that year and witnessed the memorable events that led to the overthrow of the Communist regime, which many thought would survive, along with the East German government. Apparently the sight of abandoned cars left behind by East Germans who had managed to clamber over the walls to refuge in the West German embassy was a significant factor in the demonstration that toppled the Czech regime.

In February 1989, 100 cuttings came, together with the appropriate phytosanitary certificate. Dr Ing Chmelař came later. He travelled extensively through many of the UK's most famous arboreta and wrote a most effusive letter of thanks. I don't know how often

Above The cones of the Burmese spruce *Picea farreri*. *Right* Our rare *Picea farreri*.

Modern Italian seat in 1980 with the yew hedge around it...

...and as we first saw it.

The seat flanked by mature planting now.

Left Hermes in 2015. *Above* Hermes in the early 1980s.

Primulas with *Arisaema* in the background on the damper ground.

Above Arisaema tortuosum. Right Salix gracilistyla 'Melanostachys'.

he had emerged from the rigours of life behind The Iron Curtain but he'd shown little enthusiasm about going back. We were soon pursued by phone calls from friends and contacts who, after he'd stayed with us, had invited him to visit for a night or so. They were having trouble persuading him to move on. The collection remains substantially intact to this day. One of my favourite plants is the black willow (*Salix gracilistyla* 'Melanostachys') with its black catkins; and it is difficult to ignore the Japanese fantail willow (*Salix udensis* 'Sekka') with its extraordinary fasciated stems which are fused so that they look flat.

We learned many more lessons making the water features I've talked about in this chapter, and in others. To summarise: we've dammed Marston Brook to create five new ponds; we have built the Rill with its thirty-six fountains; we have restored one lake and created two more; we have restored three fishponds, a canal and the old village pond; and we've built a system to harvest the rain water

from our greenhouses and ancillary buildings into one 16,000-litre and two 12,000-litre galvanised water tanks so it can be recycled.

We have learnt that water is not easily tamed. It has a mind and purpose of its own. It knows where it wants to go and will pursue its intentions unremorsefully. With hindsight, many other things we discovered are blindingly obvious. One: access is important so it's best to avoid steep sloping sides. Two: weed suppressant plants can be helpful and there are herbaceous perennials that can hold their own – *Gunnera*, *Rheum palmatum*, *Podophyllum*, *Rodgersia* and hostas are conspicuous in our plantings. Three: avoid invasive bamboos like the plague. Check before you buy; not all species are invasive. We are in the process of extracting massive bamboo roots stretching up to thirty-five feet from the original clumps. Four: we are also reducing the areas of marginal planting by eliminating narrow strips to let the grass cutters get to the water's edge.

Helped by our plentiful supply of clay, we have built many dams. We learnt that the thicker we make them the more successful they are. The first years, of course, are trouble-free. Memories of the tiny stream creeping up the sides of the infant pond are indelible. The American crayfish will share your excitement. They have new homes, new food and new playgrounds, with no thought of gratitude as they burrow remorselessly into your dam. Roots of growing trees or shrubs can, if allowed or wrongly-planted, weaken the dam's strength. And with winter will come the flood that sweeps over the dam and weakens it on both sides. At first you may not notice the tiny trickle beneath a stone or within some marginal shade. Act when you see it: it will get bigger. Whatever the material – stone, concrete, metal shuttering – every dam has two ends and a bottom where it meets the natural soil. Vigilance and plenty of winter attention is our advice. Those trickles are in a hurry and have all the force of nature behind them. That's why each of our ponds has its own overflow to cope with winter flooding.

Some people ask if we had a master plan for our water projects. No, we didn't. If there had been one, we might have sought professional advice and anticipated problems that were to arise. Ironically, some of the professionally designed projects spawned the most difficult problems. And a master plan would have raised questions of cost that might have undermined our enthusiasm. So these schemes emerged over the years as ideas and opportunities presented themselves. Looking back, there were mistakes but no regrets.

Of course, water is the making of the garden: your own nature re-serve, a personal therapy, every note in harmony with its background, a mirror for the colour, shape and drama of the things you've planted. If only there was time to stop and enjoy it. But of course there isn't. Gardens are living things: improvements have to be made, mainte-nance needs to be carried out. And then there is the next expansion…

Water in gardens is priceless if you want to create an impact-ful landscape – it has created breathtaking beauty from the earliest times. Italy's fountains, France's chateaux… the sweep of history's water-filled landscapes are inspirations to us all.

Chapter Six

JEAN'S WOOD, THE LAKE & THE FISHPONDS

In a massive task, a wide variety of trees, shrubs and waterside plants – arranged
around meandering paths and short avenues – recreate a flavour of Thenford's past.

by Michael Heseltine

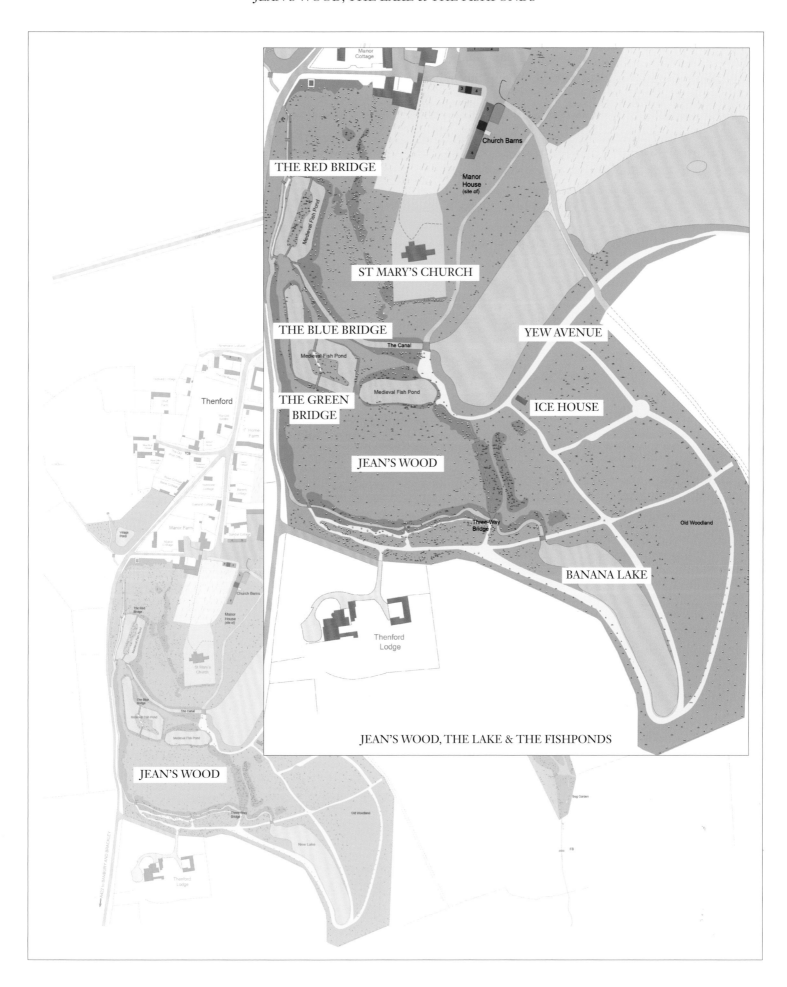

THE RED BRIDGE

ST MARY'S CHURCH

THE BLUE BRIDGE

YEW AVENUE

THE GREEN
BRIDGE

ICE HOUSE

JEAN'S WOOD

BANANA LAKE

JEAN'S WOOD, THE LAKE & THE FISHPONDS

JEAN'S WOOD

WHEN WE MOVED INTO THENFORD and Jean Summers relocated to Thenford Lodge, just beyond St Mary's church, she kept the twenty-five acres of woodland there. Ever since, they have been known as Jean's Wood.

Centuries ago, St Mary's and the mediaeval manor house and fishponds clustered near it at the southeastern corner of the village would have been Thenford's focal point. Over the centuries, our western stream, which flows there, served as the village sewer. It also provided a spur – *well clear of its earlier use!* – that runs through the fishponds and osier beds, where the willows for making baskets and fishtraps were grown. The Victorians made ornamental features out of the fishponds and built a one-and-a-half-acre bathing pond by creating a canal off the top-most fishpond and taking a feed from it to supply the second and third ponds.

We know, from the 1851 OS map mentioned earlier, how the fishponds were laid out. We know little of the old manor house except that it was originally mediaeval then later refurbished during the reign of Elizabeth I. Oak panelling was preserved and reused in the top floor bedrooms of our house. It is also possible that some

of the manor house stone was used to build a milking parlour, while the keystone is now built into the bridge at Bridge Pond. We have converted the milking parlour into cottages and a facility for domestic and commercial use. Originally there was a mill close by, on the other side of the lane. An old farm worker told us he remembers it being demolished as late as the 1920s.

If this description draws a picture of an orderly arrangement of historic perspective, it is highly misleading. When we arrived, a double line of yews – a yew avenue – to the east of the lake was impenetrable. The site of the manor was unmarked. The milking parlour was derelict. The bathing pond was but a six-inch deep puddle. You could walk across the silted-up fishponds and the canal that fed the lake if you battled through infestations of butterbur (*Petasites hybridus*). The only way to detect the ponds' location was by the shallows in the soil and the rushes and by checking the 1851 map which showed their original outline. A handful of larch and several rows of ash were the only evidence of human activity.

We knew that, when this part of the property eventually became ours, we would face the massive task of not only removing

The silted-up bathing pond.

the vast range of self-seeded trees and shrubs but also the debris where old trees had fallen and invasive undergrowth had taken hold. There had of course been a battle for survival of the fittest. Whatever wind and bird had delivered created a jungle of the strongest. However, there is much to be said for a natural wilderness: a sanctuary for wildlife; a haven of peace and solitude; and, for our predecessor, a living history of most of her life and a treasure trove of memories. We knew why Jean Summers had held on to this refuge.

Jean's son Martin came to see us in 1991 to say that his family had now decided to tidy up the arrangements that in 1976 had left them with significant properties in the village. His mother would remain in the Lodge while she lived but everything else could now come to us, leaving only the derelict farm buildings, which were under different ownership and which we did not acquire until 2005. Of course everyone had seen what we had done with the woodland we already owned. Big changes were inevitable but years later, when I drove Jean around the arboretum we had planted, she was complimentary. In 1992

The impenetrable yew avenue.

Lines of ash indicating deliberate planting.

A battle for survival.

A natural wilderness.

Fallen trees made the mess worse.

Martin was generous enough to tell us his father would have liked to have done something similar himself.

A decade earlier, as Secretary of State for the Environment, I had introduced the Wildlife and Countryside Act. Together with Tom King, the Minister of State who succeeded me, we had been responsible for a regime of environmental protection that was rigorous and effective. Indeed, I usually remain quiet as I listen to the often bitter criticisms of the politicians who introduced the present conservation regulations. There is a high chance that Tom and I were responsible. Certainly I remember a conversation in 1980 with the Royal Society for the Protection of Birds. I told them I was probably the friendliest Secretary of State they would ever have and asked what new protections they would like. At the time, magpies were quite uncommon, attracted a salute and prompted a poem. *One for sorrow, two for joy…* The consequent restraint on egg collecting has played its part in the present plague and in the consequent decimation of smaller birds.

This background, however, ensured that we knew the rules. The first step was to consult widely before we could decide the historic significance of what remained in the fishponds and Jean's Wood area. In the neighbouring village of Middleton Cheney, Cliff and Joyce Christie had established a hospital for injured wildlife in their small cottage and its garden. Of their many achievements, the hand-rearing of a brood of kingfishers was the most remarkable; heavy earth-moving equipment had sliced the top off the tunnel leading to their nest. The Christies rescued the brood and fed them by personally masticating fish from local streams for their food. They were released back into the wild on our land, where kingfishers are to be seen to this day.

In October 1991 the Christies introduced us to The Wildlife Trust for Buckinghamshire, Cambridgeshire and Northamptonshire who, early the following year, did a main sites survey. The results were interesting but revealed nothing of environmental significance. In November 1991 I wrote to Thames Water Utilities, which led to a report by M. C. Crafter describing the historic and woodland features. Its introduction gave us the encouragement we hoped for –

• *A largely intact 18th century landscape still remains superimposed on a former mediaeval open field system with Manor House site with possible fishponds/lakes.*

• *The area has considerable historic landscape importance and retains sufficient features to justify restoration.*

Restoration investment would need to concentrate on:

• *Desilting of lakes and aqueduct/ditch system.*

• *Installation of new weirs and provision of water supply.*

• *Strengthening original evergreen planting with its substantial yew component.*

• *The lakes and woodland are currently of limited ecological value and, though regenerating scrubland offers some cover for song birds, this should largely be cleared to regain the 18th century character. Desilting and opening up of the lakes would produce a considerable ecological improvement, not least through raised water quality.*

• *Opening up view lines closed by recent scrub and woodland colonisation.*

Anne discussed our ideas with Gervase Jackson-Stops, Architectural Adviser to the National Trust for more than twenty years, who lived in nearby Horton. He was at that time in charge of the restoration of Stowe Park, Buckinghamshire, and suggested that we talk to the people engaged for the work there. In January 1992 we received advice from R. W. Wheeler, Regional Land Agent of the National Trust, recommending two people who could help us.

For the sluices, Mr Wheeler suggested Chris Wallis, whose very significant claim to fame was that he was the son of Barnes Wallis, the brilliant scientist who created the bouncing bombs immortalised in the film *The Dam Busters* depicting the destruction of the Mohne Dam by Guy Gibson and his flight of Lancaster bombers in May 1943. For the dredging, Mr Wheeler recommended John Atkinson, who learnt about the restoration of ancient waterways while Gervase was restoring Stowe Gardens.

Incidentally, it was only when rereading the correspondence for this book that we noticed that in his letter Mr Wheeler referred to the £11.3m cost of the works of Stowe. It hadn't occurred to us that he might have been sending us a warning! Fortunately, we do not have the many temples and gazebos that adorn Stowe, and our bill was a fraction of theirs!

In the meantime, we had sent copies of the Thames Water report recommending comprehensive restoration to the County Archaeologist, the local county and district authorities, the National Rivers Authority and the Royal Commission on the Historical Monuments of England. The responses raised no objections to our proposals. An assessor from the Royal Commission, C. C. Taylor, described the fishponds as of local rather than national or regional significance. 'The main point of interest in the site is that it represents the process of continuous change that gives the heritage of England its importance and fascination,' he wrote. Mr C. T. Idle of English Nature felt that such work would almost certainly attract a more varied wildlife interest than currently existed. He urged us to take care of the small heronry. It still flourishes, with a brood of young every year.

The first steps towards implementation were to commission a survey which, on Chris Wallis's recommendation, was entrusted to Christopher Currie, a consultant archaeologist who had done an MPhil on the archaeology of mediaeval fishponds. The object was to re-establish the edges of the ponds and waterways and the location of the sluices. In the meantime, Wallis designed a bridge to replace the fragile contraption at the lower end of the canal where it flowed into the bathing pond and another to cover a cascade between the middle and bottom fishpond. We commissioned him to build both. Later we planted the canal banks.

John Atkinson is a master craftsman. Watching him control massive earth moving machines, it is as though his own fingers are at work, searching to distinguish between the original hard clay bottom and sides and the soft silt-based mud. He had begun by rebuilding the original sluice gate in the northwest corner where the stream entered our land. It was essential to prevent water flowing as he worked.

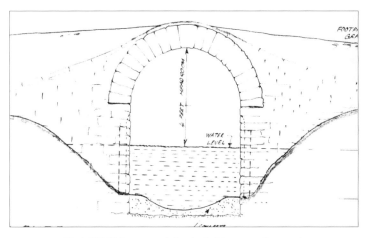

Chris Wallis's proposal for the bridge over the canal.

A fragile contraption.

The bridge over the canal under construction.

The canal banks planted.

Swans are content here. *Right* Bridge at the outlet of Middle Fishpond.

Rubble at the west end of the church wall.

Besides the restoration of the fishponds and the canal, there were specific tasks. Flooding the fishponds would have left two of them with islands and no access. We needed bridges. The original drainage system for the water works had to be rebuilt. The links between the lower ponds and over the canal were little more than concrete stepping-stones. The southern stone wall of the churchyard – close to the western side of the bathing pond – was just rubble at its western end. At the eastern end, the Severnes had built, into the old wall, a bright brick face to the family crypt.

Finally, we faced the problem of disposing of the silt. There were no obvious solutions. How deep was the silt and where was it to go? What would happen to the small roach and rudd that had survived the blistering summer of 1976? We employed specialists to stun the fish and transfer them to our new lake. We contemplated a range of Heath Robinson ideas to scoop out the silt. We ignored the suggestion in an early letter from Chris Wallis that we might dry it, bag it and sell it off to help pay for the reclamation project itself. In the event we created a sloping track into the lake from the southeast corner for earth moving equipment and a twenty-ton truck. We soon discovered that far from a six-inch puddle, we were restoring a lake three feet deep at the sides and dropping to fourteen feet in the middle. As we dredged all that silt, we hoped we might find historic souvenirs but sadly the only discovery was a *c.* eighteenth century clay pipe, albeit in perfect condition.

Two thirds of the lake's edge had a stone wall, most of which had long since been destroyed by tree roots or had collapsed into the bed and was lying where it had fallen. Through gritted teeth we decided to

rebuild it. Local building firm P. R. Alcock and Sons provided us with a stonemason and labourer on day work at £7.50 and £6.25 per hour respectively in October 1992.

Alongside the lake, we built a clay dam enclosing the bottom of a pasture slope. We used this as a holding area for the silt where it could dry and eventually be used in the arboretum. The scheme worked well but on reflection we underestimated the danger of containing liquid mud. The drying process was far too slow because the clay held the water; we should have created more effective drainage through the dam.

We should have fenced the silt tip to prevent anyone or anything wandering into it. Bill Mayo, who had lived in Thenford most of his life and had worked on the estate caring for the heavy horses, was

Remains of the original sluice on the canal.

A Heath Robinson scoop did the job of removing the silt.

delighted to see the work restoring the old ponds. He was extremely helpful too, pouring out his memories of Thenford in the 1920s and 1930s. Alas, he ventured too far into the silt and was only lucky enough to escape because there were workers nearby. But one of his wellies is buried far below – an excitement for a future archaeologist. A warning letter went to everyone in the village. Eventually the ground hardened and its extensive planting now includes an avenue of cherries. They are half of a collection of *Prunus* which originated in Matsumae, Hokkaido. The other half line the path along the Top Drive going north from our main entrance (Chapter Four).

Back to the bridges. The top and middle fishponds had islands so we decided to build two bridges to both. We invited Banbury landscape architect Robert Adams to design a number of options. We

Causeway between Jean's Lake and ours.

Tree roots destroyed the lake wall...

...which we decided to rebuild.

The enclosure made to retain the silt.

The first black silt in our holding area. In the end, it was full.

Once the silt dried, we planted an avenue of cherries over it.

couldn't reach a consensus about his three designs. We compromised by using all of them and in 1994 commissioned Martin Lilley, a local builder, to construct them at a cost of £12,000, £14,000 and £10,000. We also designed a utilitarian bridge by laying a row of flat planks on two substantial beams: totally unobtrusive, strong and serviceable. We were to use variants of this technique several times to cross waterways. They had to be strong enough to carry our golf buggy or a horse. Alongside the bridge over the canal we unearthed the remains of the original sluice. It had provided a means of draining the canal. Anne had become friendly with Oliver Impey, a Curator at the Ashmolean Museum in Oxford, whose son Edward was a mediaeval archaeologist and historian. He generously gave us a drawing that enabled us to reconstitute this sluice and three others providing us with the ability to empty each fishpond.

The second stone bridge between the two lower fishponds was particularly interesting because of the pipe that took water from the sluice in Middle Fishpond into Lower Fishpond. We found that it was a ten-foot-long oak tree trunk with a four-inch diameter hole drilled through its centre. Oak is capable of surviving underwater in good conditions and thus we were pleased to be able to re-incorporate it in the rebuilt drainage system.

The new waterworks were sufficiently advanced by my sixtieth birthday in 1993 to permit an official flooding ceremony attended by a small party of family and friends. The water in the bathing pond was crystal clear. We stocked the lake with the help of local supplier John Washbourne who provided four breeding carp and golden orfe. Within hours the cormorants were circling. Today, giant carp laze on the surface on windless sunny days, protected in part by the waterlilies (*Nymphaea* cvs.) which Sir George and Lady Young helped us plant. One extraordinary tree survives however: an ancient multi-stemmed Scots pine that was almost certainly planted to nurse the young yews at the time our house was built. Seen from the opposite side of the lake, along with a contrasting group of three golden Indian bean trees (*Catalpa bignonioides* 'Aurea'), it frames the church. A rowan (*Sorbus sargentiana*) provides the best of fruit and later autumn colour nearby.

The twenty-five acres is now largely planted with a wide variety of trees, shrubs and waterside and other herbaceous plants. Meandering paths, stream-side paths, short avenues and the yew avenue have transformed the original desolation.

It was interesting and encouraging to read the early advice that reclaiming the atmosphere of the historic waterways would enhance the food chains for wildlife and prove beneficial for conservation. There were no factual surveys so comparison with the situation today is subjective and conjectural. Leading Northamptonshire naturalist Cliff Christie wrote in May 1997 to report his findings of dragonflies on the newly restored waterways. He had spotted Large Red, Blue-

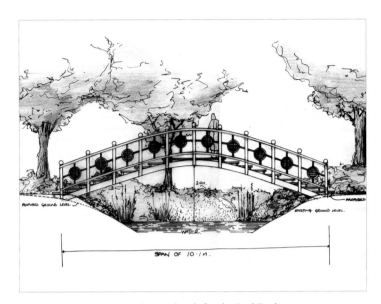

Robert Adams's sketch for the Red Bridge.

The Blue Bridge now.

The Red Bridge now.

Robert's sketch for the Blue Bridge.

Sketch for the Green Bridge.

ext page Blue Bridge goes to the island in Middle Fishpond.

The Green Bridge from Middle Fishpond's island to its south bank.

Michael's sixtieth birthday – opening the sluice.

tailed, Azure and Common Blue damselflies and, on an earlier visit, Black-tailed Skimmers and Blue Emperors. A visiting bat expert, Lawrence Armstrong, who came in 2015, believed that in addition to our population of common pipistrelle, soprano pipistrelle, brown long-eared, noctule and Daubenton's bats, the existence of so much water could be responsible (although it was unconfirmed) for whiskered, Brandts and Natterer's.

The colony of herons of concern to Mr Vole is still in place. But it would be wrong to claim progress in birdlife. A pair of Canada geese that excited us by their arrival on our new lake in 1979 is now a flock of more than 200 and the water bird diversity has suffered. The explosion in grey squirrels (see Chapter Fourteen) is much worse. To protect our rare trees and nesting birds, we concluded that we had to cull.

In the second half of 2015 we carried out our own bird survey which created a list of about eighty species we've seen on our land over the years. We take pleasure in knowing that the arboretum provides a long and varied food supply.

An eighteenth century ice house built into the bank on the southeastern side of the bathing pond is now restored, and secured to ensure no adventurous child disappears into its sixteen-foot well.

The new sluice in Top Fishpond.

Survivor: the multi-stemmed Scots pine.

Sorbus sargentiana.

End of the original wooden drain.

The yew avenue was cleared and grassed. On the opposite bank, the church wall is rebuilt and matching stone disguises the brick-faced mausoleum. Mistakes certainly. Bamboos can be slow to start but once underway throw up their shoots wider and stronger by the season. As I noted in Chapter Five, they are tough to eradicate. They evoke tales of a Chinese torture where someone is tied spread-eagled on the ground over the pin-sharp, steel-strong bamboo shoots that will eventually grow through their bodies. Best avoided. We have learned that dwarf elder (*Sambucus ebulus*) is invasive and voracious – kill it!

The slow but relentless build-up of new silt deposits since our reclamation has been more ominous and difficult to watch. Twenty-three years ago, as we wandered across the ponds' silted-up surfaces, we could not know how long they had taken to silt up in the first place. It was perhaps ten years before we realised that autumn leaves and sediment were making the lake and ponds silt up all over again. In 2015, twenty years after our restoration, we cleared the canal. We had to remove up to two feet of silt, which had left only about a foot of increasingly weed-infested water. With a large excavator and a dumper truck, the work took a week. We were lucky to have old quarry workings close by on our land to absorb the liquid mess.

Below the lowest fishpond the surplus water flows to join up with

Previous page Catalpa bignonioides 'Aurea' frame the church. *Above* The Yew Avenue now.

The ice house.

The site of the Banana Lake.

The Banana Lake today.

the original stream. We designed a wooden bridge to cover the small pool where they meet. The unified stream then runs southeast to a small stone bridge and along a gently curving valley. Higher up, on a gradual and considerable slope to the east, there's a badger colony and a wooded area that serves as a graphic reminder of Thenford as it was in 1976 and probably for centuries before that. The lie of the land and the elegance of the curve below the spinney have their own eloquence.

I suppose it was obvious what the conversation was about when Anne and I saw Darren Webster, our Head Gardener, and John Atkinson in discussion down there. We needed another lake! Its shape became banana-like so it is called Banana Lake. We sought permission with the help of Roger Balmer and consulting civil engineers Adam Power Associates. It was granted after some hesitation. The advertisement required by the Water Resources Act 1991 announcing our intention to obstruct or impede the flow of an inland water by impounding works appeared in the *Banbury Guardian* on 9 February 2006. To satisfy the Environment Agency, we had also to conduct a flood risk assessment of the consequences should the dam burst. The surplus soil was no problem. It was used for the dam and to landscape the surrounding area.

Another sluice and a major drain and – despite delay caused by heavy snow – three months later Thenford had a significant new water feature with, to its west, pastureland and a recently-planted hedge ten yards from its edge. We replanted some of the self-seeded yews widely available from our clearings. There was no sophistication about transplanting them. Earth moving equipment dug a large hole then the bucket scooped up a yew – often ten to fifteen feet high – with as much root as possible. After staking each, and with careful watering until regrowth seemed well underway, we had very few casualties. Nine years later we have a screen of healthy yews backed by a line of red maple cultivars (*Acer rubrum* cvs.) that one day will give dramatic autumn colour and contribute to a substantial shelter built against the prevailing southwesterly winds.

When this additional work below Jean's Wood had been finished, we had extended the arboretum by ten acres. We planted with an eye to the future, which is very boring: trees are identified by their mature size and look lonely and exposed when nothing is planted closer than thirty or forty yards. Without protective cover, they are not helped by exposure to the winds. The new trees are in for a lonely few years before saplings become small trees or larger bought-in specimens recover from the shock and put on new growth. Slowly, the future pattern emerges but patience and some imagination are required. We probably should have planted a thicket of disposable nurse trees – Christmas trees for the marketplace?

Left St Mary's from the north side. *Above* One of Thenford's most charming views, from the ice house to St Mary's.

Chapter Seven

THE SCULPTURE GARDEN

Preparing the site and designing an outdoor sculpture gallery where the theme is
'Modern British' but a monumental Lenin tends to shock and surprise.

by Anne Heseltine

THENFORD
The Creation of an
English Garden

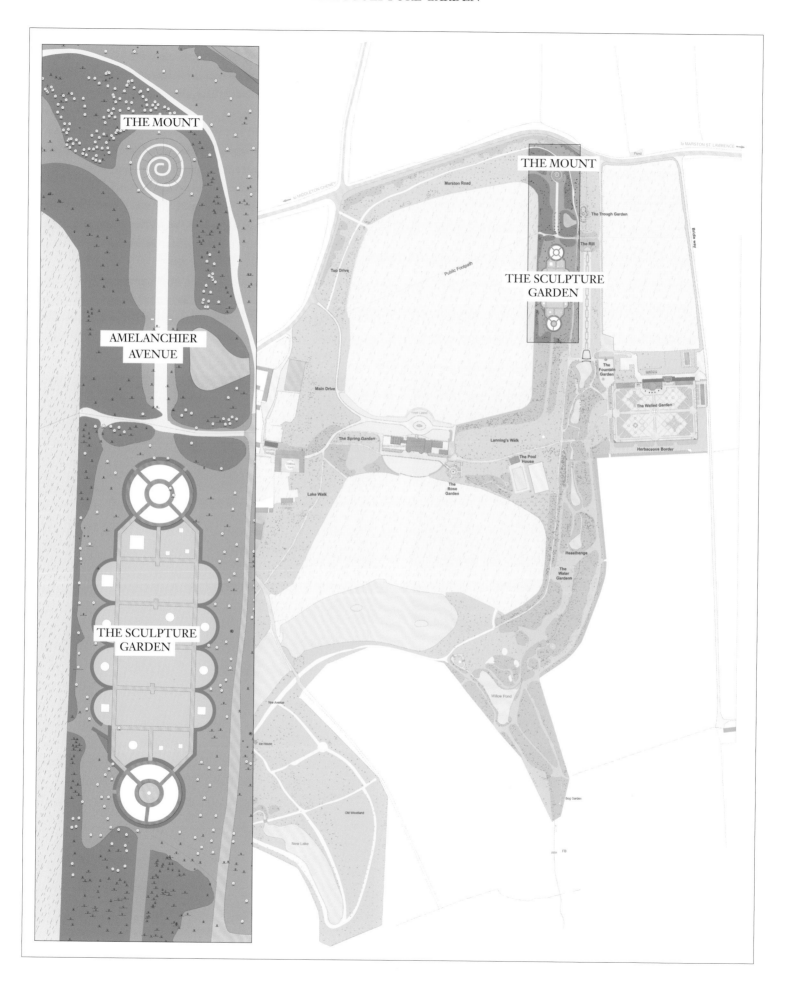

WE LEFT THE 1984 TORY PARTY CONFERENCE in Brighton after Michael's speech at lunchtime on Thursday, 11 October. Our last conversation was a brief word with an old friend, Tony Berry, MP for Enfield Southgate. We flew to Italy and stayed overnight in Stresa in readiness for one of the regular NATO conferences of defence ministers next day. Early that morning – we were still in bed – Michael's Private Secretary, Richard Mottram, awoke us with terrible news. The IRA had bombed the Grand Hotel in Brighton. Tony Berry had been killed and his wife Sarah, a very dear friend of mine, had been buried in the rubble. Thank God she was later rescued. She had a fractured pelvis but her life was intact. Four others had been killed.

We had planned, in the time available before returning home, a visit to one of Italy's largest tree nurseries, Peverelli, near Como. Despite the circumstances, we decided to go ahead with our visit. The nursery had been selected by the Italian government to provide the trees for Italy's contribution to Liverpool's International Garden Festival in 1984. Michael had announced the plans for the festival in 1979 after he became Secretary of State for the Environment and was responsible for introducing garden festivals to the UK. They featured predominately in his policies for urban regeneration. In October 1984, at the end of the festival, Italy's magnificent oaks, hornbeams, spruce and pines were still growing on the bank of the Mersey. The nursery's owner asked if we would like them because they were reluctant to bring them home. Overwhelmed by this generosity, we accepted without out checking what it would cost to move these giants from Liverpool to Thenford. Today, virtually all of them still flourish with us.

During the same visit we bought thirteen cone shaped yews, about six feet tall, to make a circle at the northern end of Lanning's Walk. My idea was to create a knot garden within this circle because I had always loved them as a design element.

It was a parliamentary colleague of Michael's, Robert Jackson, MP for Wantage, who, as soon as he saw the little trees while he was walking around the garden with me, suggested that they should be grown into a circular wall with archway openings and a flat top. To

The yew cones in 1987.

Yews planted in groups of five in the north circle.

Metal frame used to train the yews into an arch.

Anne, the tazza fountain and two fastigiate oaks from Liverpool.

South circle, tazza fountain and box plants.

South knot garden with pots to hold buckets.

South knot garden with tazza pool and sculpture.

Erecting the tazza fountain.

ensure identical size of the arches, we made a metal frame around which we trained the yew. We added weeping silver pears (*Pyrus salicifolia* 'Pendula') that sprawled over the top. We later replicated this circle at the other end of the Sculpture Garden. This time, professional advisors told us to plant five yews in place of the singleton in our earlier version. The results are indistinguishable, even if it took longer originally.

In the house, I reigned! But Michael was always king in the garden because his knowledge of plants was better than mine. Although we planned designs together, I always bowed to his plantsmanship. In our earliest days, it had been different. We walked around the jungle that was to become the arboretum. I had been brought up in the country, in the Chilterns, a thickly wooded area, and my mother was pretty good on trees and wild flowers, so Michael expected me to name all the trees. Of course, I didn't use Latin like the best gardeners but I had a reasonable knowledge. We passed sycamores, oaks, ashes, holly, firs and pine trees, wonderful huge limes (the remains of an avenue),

The cleared space with one beech still.

The layout for the Sculpture Garden. *Right* The northern knot garden.

and finally came to a hornbeam. Michael's trust in me faltered. 'That's what sailors used to dance in the Georgian navy!' he said. Since then, despite the dyslexia that still dogs him, he has learnt all the Latin names and, what's more, understands what *serrata*, *quercifolia* and *alternifolia* actually mean. I admire this very much. Although he passed Latin at School Certificate he is not comfortable with other languages. He has applied himself doggedly to the names because he loves the plants they represent.

Finally, I crossed the boundary: I designed and filled a sculpture garden. We did not have the space for sculpture in the house, and I was concerned that the wooden floors, not always absolutely level, might find the weight of bronze or stone too much. So my sculpture gallery had to be in the garden.

I started with a clean sheet. A large lawn had been created by the removal of endless sycamore saplings and one or two large beeches. Michael Severne, who'd been so helpful and kind when I was researching the estate and house, told me that he and his brother, as boys, were commissioned by their father to plant young trees in long lines, nine paces apart. They had planted ash trees down by the fishponds, and here they were larch. At any rate, they were not grown for their beauty or botanical interest!

In our early days at Thenford I haunted the salerooms, looking for furniture, works of art for the house or simply interesting eye catchers for the garden. Our political life was always interfering with these treasure hunts, but I found the auction house staff very accommodating. Elizabeth Lane, of Christie's, took me to view a country house sale near Marlow before it was ready for the public. A large many-beamed house immediately suggested Noel Coward weekend parties. We knocked on the front door, which was opened by a young man in a white cable-knit sweater with a coloured border to its neckline. Without thinking, I blurted out: 'Anyone for tennis?' Fortunately, he laughed too. It was a successful viewing: not only did I leave a bid on a wonderful white marble fountain, in the form of a tazza, but in a rather unpromising shed I found a beautiful little Georgian birdcage. Later, I was to find its twin in a sale at Sotheby's.

We set up the marble fountain from the 'Noel Coward' house in the circle of yews, by now trimmed and grown into a colonnade of arches. Within the circle, the Knot Garden was formed in box hedging: two types – one dark and one light – weaving over and under each other, with topiarised yews in the beds, growing out of a floor of pink granite chippings. The pink chippings were inspired by a visit to the Villa Lante near Viterbo, Italy, and they are so much prettier than the usual grey. Beyond this circle, we cleared and levelled a flat site and I designed a series of 'rooms', with beech hedging, each ending in a semi-circular area that was to house a substantial sculpture. This way, you could only see the contents of any room at one time, so there would be no jarring of styles – very contemporary sculpture could live happily in the next room to eighteenth century pieces. I am not an architect so my rather amateurish drawings had to be transformed into a professional plan. We were lucky to be recommended to Ban-

Above left The gloriette in a French junkyard. *Above right* Giant vessel by Maryanne Nicholls. *Right* Etiolated couple by Derek Howarth.

bury landscape architect Robert Adams (a name to live up to, despite the 's'). He elaborated on my initial plan and somehow achieved a flat, dry area. As Michael mentioned in the previous chapter, Robert also designed bridges for us over the fishponds, including the 'Monet' bridge, and the Japanese bridge.

As it turned out, virtually all the Sculpture Garden's works are contemporary, or what is loosely known as 'Modern British'. At the north end is a second circular knot garden that focuses on a gloriette, or gazebo, which we found in rusty condition in a roadside junkyard in France. It is made from painted iron work, which was at first dark red but has now faded to a somewhat washed out pink. It will probably remain this colour because the complications of unwinding the vines (*Vitis vinifera* 'Müller-Thurgau' and *V. vinifera* 'Purpurea') entwined on it are too horrid to contemplate. The vines produce large bunches of grapes in summer that, rather disappointingly, taste very sour – even the birds reject them. However, in 2015 our chef, Henry Mayo, rather optimistically put some on the lunch table and we found them delicious. But that was an exceptional year.

As you enter the garden from the south, the etiolated couple in the first knot garden remind me of the ancient Egyptian couples in the British Museum, which I always find rather touching: the man always has an arm around the woman's shoulders. I bought them in Ludlow on a shooting trip to Wales. They are by Derek Howarth.

The first two sculptures on the right are from Cambodia. We travelled to Siem Reap one year to visit the temples of Angkor Wat, Angkor Thom and many others. These are the temples that were covered in creepers and overgrown with trees, all but forgotten for many, many years until the wars that rampaged in that area in the 1980s brought them to light again. Near the temple complex is a sculpture school, where the students learn to recreate the works that were vandalised during the wars, or later stolen by tourists or opportunist dealers. The sculptures also suffer from erosion. Many are carved from soft sandstone which eventually deteriorates. To fund their work, the school will make facsimiles of any piece that takes your eye, provided you take a decent photograph of it. We photographed two massive heads now known in the family as Mr Grumpy and Mr Smiley – for

Preparing the site for 'Standing Man'...

...and Ken Cook installing him.

The Minotaur by Michael Ayrton.

obvious reasons. I had to change the label on them after I overheard two elderly ladies deploring our 'vandalism'. They had assumed that we had somehow removed the Cambodian originals. The label now reads '*Copies* of heads from Angkor Wat'. We also have a third piece: a guardian dog or lion that looks down over the Sculpture Garden from the top of the Mount. The pieces of sculpture are very mixed. Mostly, they are by young artists. I bought many from galleries in Aldeburgh, where I attend the music festival every June. Among them are the giant vessel, made in the unusual medium of slate and fibreglass, by Suffolk sculptor Maryanne Nicholls.

We have a small group of very distinguished modern British works. 'Standing Man' by Elisabeth Frink dominates the whole collection because it is the only piece on the central axis of the garden. I think this is my favourite. I have always admired Frink so much: her work has so much power and, even in a static pose such as this, breathes force and energy. The man's hands, folded behind his back, are cast from Frink's own. They are huge and dwarf mine and Michael's. We were lucky enough to meet Ken Cook, who worked

for many years as Frink's assistant and did some of her casting. He installed this and other pieces for us, and told me the story.

The second piece in this area is the Minotaur by Michael Ayrton, a work in bronze that was sculpted for a recreation of the Cretan Labyrinth in New York State, and cast in an edition of five. I had bought a drawing of a baby Minotaur by Ayrton some years before from Christopher Hull's gallery in Motcomb Street, Belgravia, so was delighted to find this Minotaur in Sotheby's.

An early work by Lynn Chadwick is called 'Two Watchers'. A couple face each other but their heads are shaped like blank boxes: the work dates back to the 1950s when television first entered peoples' homes on a wider scale and began to numb the minds of a large proportion of the populace. I must say that this was a lucky buy. We had seen it in the sale room and intended to at least watch the way the bidding went. But the day before the sale, we had bought something else and phoned Christie's to explain we would not be bidding. Halfway through lunch on the day of the sale the phone went and Michael answered it. He listened to the bidding. Fortunately, the price was on

Above and right 'Reading Chaucer' by Philip Jackson.

'Two Watchers' by Lyn Chadwick.

the low side. He came back with a big smile on his face.

Animals play a large part in the collection. They seem at home in their outdoor habitat, and fit better into this ambiance than they would in a house. We have a rather flirtatious 'Nanny Goat' by Angela Hunter, which I found in Aldeburgh: she is making eyes at a billy, entitled 'Old English Billy Goat', by Dido Crosby. A pony, rolling onto its back and rather inappropriately lying opposite a huge bust of Lenin, is entitled 'Rolling Horse'. It is by Lucy Kinsella. We also have a very elegant greyhound by Nicola Hicks, most reminiscent in style of her wire sculptures but more durable because it is cast in bronze. He has a delightfully tongue-in-cheek title: 'Nice Little Earner'.

One of our best-known British contemporary sculptors, Philip Jackson, is also represented. His recent work at Hyde Park Corner – a memorial to Bomber Command – and his statue of the late Queen Mother, Elizabeth, in the Mall, are passed by thousands of Londoners and tourists each day. They might be surprised to see 'Reading Chaucer', an elegant young lady seated on a bench reading from a heavy tome. She wears a simple mediaeval gown and a tall pointed head-

Left 'Continuum' by Cathy Lewis. *Above* 'Momentum' by Cathy Lewis.

dress. A deliciously dainty little foot points out from under the hem of the garment. In the last hedged enclosure there is a trio of sculptures by Cathy Lewis. Executed in the early 2000s, they are gymnasts, graceful and controlled, small in scale but quite perfect.

The biggest 'crowd puller' is the monumental head of Lenin that once stood on the roof of the KGB building in Preili, Latvia. It was sculpted by distinguished Latvian artist Dzintra Jansone and removed from its perch after the fall of Communism. We have given Lenin a brick wall as a plinth to remind him of his origins. Some visitors think this emblem of Communism is a symbol of my political beliefs! I have even received anonymous letters telling me how shocking it is. I see it differently. In the early days of the USSR, no private individual could adorn his home or garden with sculpture. The only patron was the state. The only outlet for artists was to reflect ideology in their work. There was no choice of subject.

When my daughter Alexandra and I visited the USSR in 1982 we were fascinated by the sculptures of the early Communist era. It was all around us, in the squares, on the buildings and even in the parks,

where romantic statues of the young Lenin in a flowing frockcoat – *and with hair!* – were more Byronic than Communist. There were handsome young men, bare-chested (Putin would have been envious) gazing boldly into the new future and flourishing a hoe or a scythe. Alongside these heroes of the state were young women with flowing hair, waving a flag or carrying a child.

Later, on another visit to Russia at the time of Glasnost and Perestroika, I was sad to see in the papers and on TV these works of art being pulled down and crushed to pulp. The work of a generation of artists was being wilfully destroyed – for idealistic reasons, and not for its lack of artistic value. I was determined to save at least one for our collection. On a later visit to Russia, when Michael was reporting for the BBC on the 1988 Reagan/Gorbachev talks, I recognised a Sotheby's executive at Moscow airport. I ran over and asked him what was happening to the disappearing sculptures. He reassured me that the best were being retained and stored temporarily in the Moscow Riding School manège, a wonderful neoclassical building built as a riding academy. A year or two later, a Sotheby's catalogue arrived out of the

Previous page Lenin being lowered into place. *Above* Lenin no doubt at home in the snow.

A rather different setting from a KGB HQ.

blue – and there was Lenin, among all the garden seats, lead shepherd-esses, lions and peacocks. We had to have him but I was in bed with 'flu. I begged Michael to go to the sale room in Sussex and view this archetypal revolutionary sculpture. We bought him. He is huge, about nine feet high, and not to everyone's taste. It was years later that we discussed the answer to the frequent question about how he turned up in a sale of garden statuary in Billingshurst, Sussex. Apparently a British dealer was in Latvia shortly after The Wall came down and was asked by local citizens, who had taken it down, if he would buy it. He phoned the auctioneer who advised him of its scrap value for the metal. On that basis he bought it, and it came up for sale whence he made a significant profit!

Two works by Ronald Rae, the distinguished Scottish sculptor, are also a delight. The first is sad and solemn: the decapitated head of John the Baptist, carved painstakingly in Creetown granite from the Solway Firth, without the use of electric drills or other gadgets. Ronald works only with the age-old tools of hammer and chisel. It can take him more than a year to complete such a work. The second is the

'John the Baptist' by Ronald Rae.

'Wounded Elephant' arriving.

'Wounded Elephant' also by Ronald Rae.

'Wounded Elephant', a monumental sculpture. These great animals sink to their knees when dying. This is that moment. The granite, which Ronald found in Kemnay Quarry in Aberdeenshire, is grey but a line of reddish striation trickles down from the elephant's eye. Is she weeping? Ronald, a giant of a man with a bushy beard – once black, now white – came to Thenford to see her safely installed. She weighs twelve tons so a temporary track had to be laid across the front park, a fence removed, two small trees uprooted and subsequently replanted to give the delivery lorry access to her site. A significant length of yew hedging had to be lifted. All of this was carried out in summer, when the plants required constant watering. Ronald was very emotional about parting with her. I invited him to visit whenever he wished but he demurred, saying that this was goodbye.

In the northern knot garden there is a set of Four Seasons – in limestone and quite new; they're from one of the many stonemasons' yards around Vicenza, northern Italy, but follow a much earlier design. As you leave this knot garden, you climb up a bank (mistake! – there should be steps) and see ahead of you the Mount. The short but

Top Pond – not as sinister as we thought.

Amelanchier Avenue looking south from the Mount...

Dealing with bamboo roots.

wide path to it is lined with *Amelanchier canadensis* – hence its name: Amelanchier Avenue. These large shrubs have a double value: they bloom pinky-white in spring and rise out of a mass of white crocus – 6000 of them! In autumn, their leaves turn a blazing scarlet.

To the right of the Amelanchier Avenue is a strange little pond called Top Pond. It was dank and unexciting, and surrounded by un-likely myths. I was told it was very deep and not to let the children near it – in fact, it was said to be so deep that a horse and cart had fallen into it, never to be seen again! We approached it warily, in wad-ers but, growing bolder, we found ourselves in the middle – with wa-ter barely knee high. It has a firm ironstone bottom, and acts as an overflow pond for the stream, but is also fed by springs. Its slightly sinister aspect is now swept away, and its upper banks are planted with *Geranium*, *Aquilegia*, *Hemerocallis*, *Heuchera* and *Hosta* cultivars. We op-timistically planted bamboo but, as usual, it bossily took over and we have removed it.

The Avenue ends with a pair of snarling tigers, brought back from a holiday in Bali. Two redbuds (*Cercis canadensis* 'Forest Pansy') plant-

...Amelanchier Avenue looking north to the Mount.

Stone tigers from Bali.

Cercis canadensis 'Forest Pansy'.

Cambodian guardian lion.

Ulmus 'Sapporo Autumn Gold'.

Amelanchier canadensis show off their autumn colour.

ed to the sides of the tigers are among the most spectacular plantings in this part of the garden. While they are interesting for their young spring foliage, they are spectacular in the autumn. *Rhododendron* 'Cunningham's White', a gift from John and Penny Gummer (Lord and Lady Deben) for Michael's 75th birthday, is lime-tolerant here, too. It is grafted onto lime-tolerant stock discovered in a German quarry.

Mounts were early devices in old gardens. There is one at Kew and another at New College, Oxford. What prompted me to think of one was the excess earth that came from levelling the ground for the Sculpture Garden. The Mount has a spiralling path to its summit, edged in box, and is surmounted by the guardian lion, which came from Cambodia. From the summit you can look down on the Sculpture Garden. In the past, mounts were built much higher so that the ladies of the household could look down on the hunt in the elegantly laid-out woodland with *allées* radiating out in a star.

Just before we came to Thenford, Dutch Elm Disease was reported to have killed more than fifteen million of Britain's mature elms. Pitney Bowes, the American shipping and mailing company, launched a campaign called 'Elms Across Europe' to provide trees to replace this carnage. These were a different species of elm (*Ulmus* 'Sapporo

Autumn Gold'). Their project was enabled by the work of Professor Eugene Smalley of Wisconsin University who had propagated a Siberian elm growing in the Hokkaido University Botanic Gardens, in Sapporo, northern Japan. Michael learnt of their scheme from Maurice Mendoza, a senior official in the Department of the Environment in 1979. Michael enquired, and the company presented us with ten small trees. The site of the Mount already had three of these, and we used a tree spade to move two more into position.

Apart from the pieces I have talked about, there are many other sculptures in the Sculpture Garden, and the rooms are now full. Visitors all have their favourites, and I usually spend a lot of time on our open days talking about them. Some visitors come every year to view a particular favourite, which is very rewarding. The entire collection is listed in the Appendix at the end of this book.

But our sculpture is not limited to the confines of the Sculpture Garden. There are the two Taplin cormorants overlooking the rear ha-ha on the south lawn; a magnificent stag by an unknown Russian artist that appears, appropriately, from a clump of conifers at the end of the Birchway; and, perhaps the most loved of all, the two hounds that guard the front of the house.

Chapter Eight

THE WALLED GARDEN

From sad neglect to two acres of magnificence where the formal setting features fruit cages,
herb garden, aviary, mirror pools, domes, a cottage ornée and a spectacular fountain.

by Michael Heseltine

THENFORD
The Creation of an
English Garden

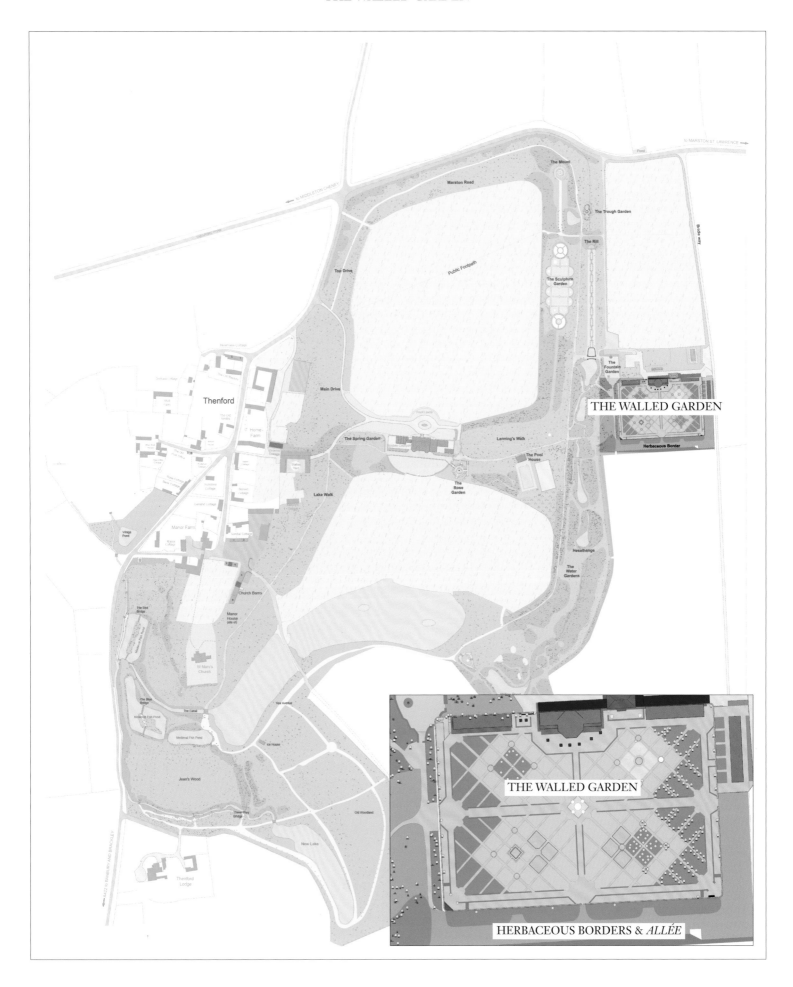

THE WALLED GARDEN

HERBACEOUS BORDERS & *ALLÉE*

THE WALLED GARDEN

WE FOUND AT THENFORD THE all-too-familiar and sad story of the country house walled garden in the third quarter of the twentieth century. The five gardeners had long since gone. The last, Charlie Anthony, had struggled on into the 1960s selling a variety of salad produce to nearby greengrocers. The beds that would have provided fruit, vegetables and flowers for the house and staff were untraceable. By the mid 1970s the Walled Garden had been grassed and used to rear lambs out of harm's way of the local foxes. Outside, two acres were given over to growing Christmas trees in a further attempt to pay bills. Sadly, Charlie pointed out to us the few remaining espaliered fruit trees with their indented lead labels, memorials to a bygone age.

The Walled Garden is large in relation to Thenford House. Its wall – brick with stone capping – encloses a magnificent two-acre rectangle. The corners are curved and without buttresses. Originally each side had a wooden gate within a designed brick surround, three of which remained when we arrived. In the east wall, a much larger functional gate that could cope with the demands of modern machinery had replaced the original. Inside, a classic, wooden-framed, lean-to

nineteenth century greenhouse made by Boulton and Paul of Norwich stood against the north wall. Its interior door led to the potting sheds and outside to the working area. There was a second greenhouse, probably an old vine house, in the centre at the cross section of the paths.

In 1926, the house where Darren Webster lives, which Anne touched on in Chapter One, had been built into the north wall, alongside the main greenhouse. This and the unattractive east gate probably ensured that, although Thenford itself is a Grade 1 listed house, the wall itself was not listed at all.

But let's start at the beginning. We needed to recruit another gardener, renovate the accommodation, invest in new paths, repair the greenhouses and reclaim the working areas. Yet we made the same mistake as our predecessors and decided to include a commercial element to defray at least part of the costs. In 1979 we built a half-acre greenhouse just outside the Walled Garden under the delusion that the profits from selling chrysanthemums in Covent Garden would help. The oil crisis of 1973 had brought down the British government

The Walled Garden between the wars.

As we found it in 1976...

...and rather different in 2016.

and rocketed the price of oil up by 500 per cent. We should never have built the greenhouse. We were forced to acknowledge our greatest mistake and sell it.

Quinlan Terry, who was building our Palladian Summer House at the time, had very clear views about the appropriate scale and proportions of the Walled Garden's original paths. We can claim our work was a restoration but there was no evidence on which to base that claim. Quinlan's plans helped us take the first essential step along the journey to creating the Walled Garden as it is today. We built the stone-edged gravel paths to divide the garden into four equal parts. We lined each of these beds with our own box cuttings grown in sixty trays.

Restoration of the greenhouses was very much 'make do and mend'. Experience has now taught us that trying to repair and hold onto old greenhouses is negative cash flow. One frame is repaired then another goes – but for the first twenty-five years we persevered.

We produced a limited supply of flowers and vegetables for the house while the rest of the area served as a nursery for trees and shrubs purchased or propagated for the arboretum. We purchased a utilitarian Cambridge greenhouse, erected a shade tunnel and laid out standing beds. The space was greatly underused despite the significant number of trees and shrubs lined out and awaiting transfer to the arboretum. It was amateurish but therapeutic; a world far removed from the flow of ministerial red boxes and the pressures of politics.

After the 1997 election, I returned to Haymarket whose horticultural publishing and agricultural businesses were growing. Before long the group purchased a significant German publishing company in the sector. We decided to raise our game. We set out to create a garden that would provide even more impressive support and background to our commercial ambitions. From the beginning, of course, appropriate agreements had been reached with HM Revenue & Customs.

The Walled Garden was a good place to start. A freak storm precipitated the first decision by blowing out a large part of the lean-to greenhouse. Following a meeting at the 1998 Chelsea Flower Show, we reached agreement with Alitex, who work with the National

The original Boulton and Paul greenhouse.

The Quinlan Terry paths.

The house in the wall soon after we arrived.

Make do and mend.

Trust and the Royal Botanic Gardens, Kew, for them to build a new south-facing feature greenhouse on the northern wall. We abandoned the old houses.

We were attracted to Alitex's greenhouses for several reasons. They have a modular system with the flexibility to fit virtually any available space. The basic material is a plastic-coated aluminium in a wide range of colours that offers a maintenance free long-term future. The traditional design is appropriate to an historic walled garden. The interior fittings are based on early Victorian designs. Even so, it was a surprise to watch the foundations take shape with something of the scale and complexity of a nuclear bunker. The greenhouse's regime demands a computer and boiler room to cope with its environmental controls. Installing the Alitex greenhouse was a brave but immensely rewarding decision that took our gardening into new realms.

But the most decisive moment concerning the Walled Garden occurred at the following year's Chelsea Flower Show when our half-formed desire to do something significant about the Walled Garden took shape. Anne and I were looking at a show garden designed by George Carter, whose work is inspired by the simple geometry of seventeenth century gardens. He is particularly interested in the structure, planting and architecture of the formal garden. In the show garden, he had installed a replica of the Florentine Etruscan boar standing on a plinth, reflected in a long, narrow pool bordered by pleached limes. We owned a pair of rococo sculptures of putti in the style of Clodion which called out for similar treatment.

We met George and invited him to help us in the context of the Walled Garden. Throughout the work, George worked with Roger Balmer, the architect who turned George's sketches into working drawings and contract documents. Planning permission for what we wanted to do was granted on 5 September 2000. We gave the building contract to Chris McDaniel, a landscaper from Suffolk with whom George had worked before. He proved not only very competitive but professional and excited by so unusual a project. At the start of the working week his six-man team would arrive in the nearby village and stay in a B&B.

In our original instructions to George we had identified a broad outline of our ambitions. The garden's four quarters would each have a purpose. We wanted a fruit cage, a sitting area, a herb garden and an

The uncommercial greenhouse.

The Cambridge greenhouse.

Shade tunnel.

Goodbye!

The new Alitex greenhouse.

The foundations for the new greenhouse.

The greenhouse's boiler room.

The domed pavilions arrive.

The Etruscan boar we saw at Chelsea Flower Show.

Our Clodion sculptures arriving.

Above The reflecting pools. *Right* The Herb Garden's central wooden pillar.

The reflecting pools and fruit cage.

aviary. The mirror pools which reflect the terracotta groups had to fit in with that outline. George designed each of the four quarters around four copper-domed pavilions. He designed two groups of three mirror pools made from black-painted fibreglass squares eighteen feet square and one foot deep. Against the background of the domes in the fruit cage and sitting area, the flooded pools would reflect our sculptures on plinths.

The herb garden, again with four domes, is divided into quarters by paved paths. The central feature, from which the paths diverge, is a wooden pillar that's home for the climbers *Rosa* 'Kathleen Harrop' and *Clematis macropetala* 'Maidwell Hall'. We drew up the planting on paper and completed our purchases by visiting the National Herb Centre at nearby Warmington. Everything was chosen for its medicinal or culinary purpose. We planted the herb garden over a Whitsun weekend and ended with backache but felt very proud of what we had achieved. Ten years later we accepted Robert Mattock's advice to plant the apothecary's rose (*Rosa gallica* var. *officinalis*) and, on eight

wire frames, a collection of climbers including *Rosa* 'Pride of Reigate', 'Captain Hayward' and 'Climbing The Queen Alexandra'.

The fruit cage with four domes is a classic of its sort. A world of berries – black-, straw-, rasp- and goose- – deliver that very best of English experiences: fruit picked fresh that day from one's own garden. It is the best way to enjoy it and far and away the most expensive!

The sitting area is the third of the centrepieces. It is built around four domes finished by four-foot high hornbeam hedges and containing a small fountain in a stone-capped raised brick water feature.

With the two-acre aviary – the folly that Anne described in Chapter Two – long gone, all that the aviculturist had left were the parakeets. But, before we built the present Aviary within the Walled Garden, it was to serve for one last time as a haven safe from the many foxes of the Bicester Country. We like peacocks and could not resist the offer of a trio of whites. I think we were influenced by their commanding presence and coarse calls on one of our country house visits. We have high walls around the house courtyards and thought

they would look nice, strutting and calling. Quite soon they moved to the Walled Garden, which presaged a remarkable sense of self-preservation. And then suddenly there were nine. The nine discovered the village and that was when the trouble began. We found little difficulty in selling the youngsters back to the dealer from where the parents had come but the parents had enjoyed the village – or, rather, any young vegetables virtually the day they sprouted or were planted out. A corpse was discovered some way away but none had any doubts about the cause of death. A fox finished off one of the hens which was stupid enough to nest outside the wall and we disposed of the survivor. Our sympathies were entirely with the villagers!

The Aviary and its four domes occupies the centre of the Walled Garden's northeast quarter. It is all that is left of the avicultural ambition that drove our first plans in 1976. Bitter experience has taught us that success requires a degree of professionalism. We found the necessary expertise to guide us in the Secretary of the Parrot Society, Les Rance. His advice was clear. Parakeets – we had now decided to

specialise – can stand the English climate but wind and damp are fatal.

Each of the Aviary domes has a fibreglass ceiling and Perspex walls with nesting boxes for the smaller species. The inhabitants have full access to three of the domes; the fourth has a double door into which you seal yourself before opening the inner door into the Aviary. Les makes a quarterly visit to supply food, check health, administer appropriate anthelmintics and if necessary replace casualties. The system works well. We have twenty-five male parakeets. A typical roll call includes Rock Peplar, Australian King, Barnard's, Rosa Bourke, Kakariki, Ring-necked, Barraband, Blue Redrump, Crimson Wing and Princess of Wales parakeets, all bred in captivity in the UK. The introduction of one female would signal the outbreak of war, with many casualties. There were inevitable mistakes. The original design included metal perches which, when frozen, caused serious problems for the parakeets' feet.

There was one rogue. A sulphur-crested cockatiel had escaped from someone's cage and arrived at Thenford one day, unannounced

The reflecting pools with the sitting area directly behind, screened by a low hedge.

Previous page The Herbaceous Borders and Walled Garden in 2016. *Above* Our male parakeets settling in to their new home.

and very tired. Anne has a collection of decorative birdcages. One, in the hall, is a large Victorian brass cage. It was made to house a full size parrot so it was a splendidly palatial home for the visitor. He throve for a few weeks and seemed content. However, a friend of ours, the painter James Reeve, who claimed to know about parrots, came to stay and advised that the cockatiel would be much happier with the other birds in the Aviary. He was duly transferred to the Aviary and seemed to fit in well. Three days later, he had killed four of his colleagues, all much rarer than him! He was removed, caged and given to a child in the village. We couldn't have a murderer in the Aviary!

The decision to build the Aviary left the question of what we should do with the functional Cambridge greenhouse. We first thought to dismantle and sell it. Then we had a better idea. Just outside the eastern wall was a small area of land where building material that 'might be useful one day' was stored. In practice, we were creating a hidden working area embracing potting sheds, growing areas, water tanks. We decided to relocate the Cambridge greenhouse there.

At the intersection of the four quarters there is a clear central space. We had greatly admired a water sculpture at Antony, Richard and Mary Carew Pole's Cornish home, when we were their guests.

Darren in the Alitex greenhouse.

Les Rance brings the parakeets to populate the new aviary.

Their family had built the house in 1721. Richard's father gave it to the National Trust in 1961. Richard and Mary commissioned William Pye to create a water sculpture in 1996, which they also gave to the Trust. Inspired by a nearby example of yew topiary, William had cleverly designed a bronze cone from the top of which a gentle flow of water pulsates and clings to its sides before disappearing into an ornate stone paving.

William, a sculptor and an engineer, had learnt as a child to love the streams near his Surrey home. After four years at the Sculpture School of the Royal College of Art and many European visits, he secured his first exhibition at the Redfern Gallery in London in 1966. His work today is featured extensively in major public displays and private collections at home and abroad. In the summer of 1999 we commissioned a sketch from him for a proposed water feature to stand at the centre of the redesigned Walled Garden. It was a bad time to choose: Bill was hard pressed to complete Millennium projects. On 14 December 1999 a letter arrived thanking us for our great forbearance and inviting us to visit his studio to look at sketches. The one that is illustrated on this page was enclosed. On 5 January 2000 we gave the go-ahead.

Idea for Thenford Walled Garden

Bill's idea for the fountain...

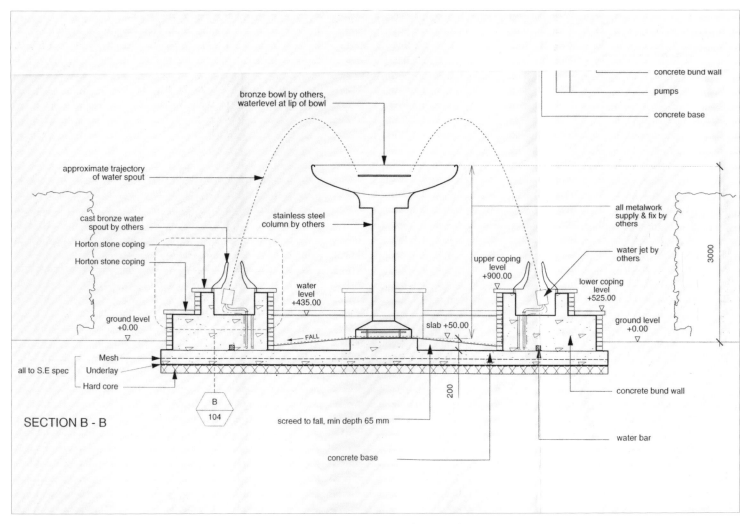

...and his working drawings for 'Coanda'.

A sketch gives no idea of the complexity involved in a construction like this. Detailed drawings like the self-explanatory one here were ready by the end of March. Bill's work is always titled. It was no surprise in June when we received a letter explaining his choice of 'Coanda'. A professor of hydraulics from Imperial College, London, had told Bill about the research by the Romanian scientist Henri Coandă into the properties of fluids clinging to surfaces. The phenomenon is known as the Coanda effect. Bill told us recently how delighted he was, while visiting Romania, to see the name Henri Coandă emblazoned across the main terminal at Bucharest airport.

The fountain is a great success. Its construction was fascinating in itself. Water jets in twelve-foot arcs from the four corners of the base into a giant bronze bowl. The water then flows over the bowl's rim, clinging to its undersides before falling in a silvery column into the pool below. At night the illuminated jets carry the light along the curve of the water. Bill is a perfectionist. A year after the fountain's completion he sent two photographs highlighting problems. One focused on the intense colour of the brick base and the other on the intrusive nature of two wooden buttresses, which were placed to frame the nearby hornbeam buttresses. There were solutions. The wooden

Darren makes the final adjustments.

Putting it together.

The crane driver was busy.

buttresses were never intended to be permanent but to give shape while the hornbeams filled out. Their task completed, they have long since gone. The brick colour certainly was in stark contrast to the cool pink of the main walls. Bill admired the colour of bricks Anne had chosen to line the herbaceous borders outside the Walled Garden. They were mellow and soft, but they were 'second-hand'. There were three possibilities. Let time take its course; rebuild the base in stone; or render the brickwork. Rebuilding in ashlar would have added £20,000 to the cost. It was possible that time would mellow the brick and its conspicuous mortar. We decided to wait and see, and still are.

The success of Bill's 'Coanda' is, of course, only to be expected. It comes from the design table of a man who has established an international reputation as a pioneer of his genre of water sculpture. It also reveals an important difference between this water project and those that have been more troublesome. 'Coanda' jets water into the air, filling its bowl and then letting it cascade into eighteen inches of water. Activated simply by the throw of a switch, it is about moving water.

The mirror pools are very different. In their two groups of three,

each individually fed, they are eighteen feet square but their water depth is just over one foot. That is no problem in winter because we drain them down, but once the temperature rises, algae develop in the slow-moving, shallow water. We have found no effective means of combatting this, other than emptying the system and physically removing the deposits. There were many suggestions but the lack of depth and movement defied them all. One of the more bizarre proposals was that we should use a black dye – apparently used in swimming pools – to give the water an intense blackness without harming people. The black dye might have coloured the buff-coloured gravel surrounds, but the discharge systems empties into one of our streams and we were deterred by the prospect of very dark water flowing on to the River Thames. In the end a solution presented itself: we treated the mirror pools like the swimming pool, with regular weekly treatment, which delivered pristine, if costly, reflections. Then we found a leak. Someone suggested, rather alarmingly, that the chemicals had eaten into the interconnecting pipework. However, since the treatment was considered safe for us to swim in, that seemed implausible.

Above The view through the wisteria arch. *Right* 'Coanda' and its elegant jets.

We had asked George Carter to place a number of other features along the walls – a wisteria arch to the west with a wall fountain at its northwest corner and an auricular theatre in the opposite corner. We wanted a picking area along the east wall. The cottage's renovation was on the list too. The process of planning the wisteria arch showed our inexperience. Instead of going straight for a handful of well-tried wisterias, we spent hours trying to design an arch with white wisteria at one end, ranging through pale and dark blue to deep purple at the other. It was a waste of time because they don't all flower at the same time. We also put in far too many individual plants, ignoring the capacity of just one to cover huge areas. In the end we settled for *Wisteria floribunda* 'Multijuga' and have replanted several of the misplaced plants in hollies in the arboretum.

Anne worked closely with George to make something of the cottage. The Snowcem had been removed as part of the work to install the first Alitex greenhouse. They replaced the awful metal windows and redesigned the house as a 'cottage *ornée*'. The idea was inspired by a book Anne owned, *Designs for Gate Lodges, Gamekeeper's Cottages,*

Plenty of mud making the pool to surround 'Coanda'.

The auricula theatre.

210

Transformation into a cottage *ornée*.

Jim Horrobin's first gate from the herbaceous border into the Walled Garden.

The view into the Walled Garden.

and other Rural Residences by T. F. Hunt, published in 1825. George drew the design and an eyesore became an asset. We then added two more simple Alitex greenhouses on either side of the domed central feature.

Anyone who has ever been involved in a construction project is all too familiar with the early destruction stages and the mess. Working outside means rain. Rain means mud and mud means delay. It was an unforgettable experience.

Among the things we wanted to do was to replace a small wooden door into the Walled Garden with an iron one. In the 1990s we had a significant anniversary approaching and Anne felt a new gate would make a splendid present. Anne was then a Trustee of the Victoria & Albert Museum. She had a close relationship with the metalwork department, and sought their advice. The curator said immediately that one blacksmith was outstanding – but that sadly he lived in a very remote place so working with him would not be practical. Casually, Anne asked where and was amused to hear that Jim Horrobin was in Porlock, a small town on the Somerset coast, only a few miles from the little farm she owned on Exmoor. She knew exactly where Jim was.

Jim's grandfather was a coppersmith and his father Harry was the village blacksmith and farrier at Bridgetown in the Exe Valley. Harry had begun the trend to ornamental ironwork which Jim was to expand. He was helped by his marriage to Gabrielle, a professional gilder and artist. She was able not only to assist with Jim's commissions but also to present them in her beautiful watercolour illustrations. Jim enjoyed an international reputation not only for his work in helping to

Jim's gate for the east wall, incorporating his heron's head pattern.

found the British Artist Blacksmiths Association in 1978 but through his commissions, including lanterns for the portico of St Paul's Chapel, Broadway, New York City – the oldest surviving church building in Manhattan – and the monumental Churchill Screen in the Crypt of St Paul's Cathedral, London.

We asked Jim for design proposals for this small gate, re-iterating that it had to be rabbit-proof. The gate he made, incorporating our initials and the date of our thirty-fifth wedding anniversary, was exactly what we'd hoped for. We were delighted and it led to a second commission.

We wanted Jim to resolve the problem of our need to get rid of that modern utilitarian gate in the east wall. (In passing, we should recognise that the gap had proved invaluable in allowing access for the pavilions: their road journey from Norfolk had had to be checked for height clearance; it was a close run thing.) We invited Jim to design a replacement. When he came to see the garden and walked through the arboretum he was impressed by the number of herons on our lakes – which gave him inspiration for his design. There was a need for an additional refinement. This is an east-facing wall so the wind would blow through open ironwork. Two transparent sliding Perspex screens solved the problem, had no effect on the view of open country and were draft proof.

As part of our planning for the Walled Garden, we had conducted a number of research visits. Before we went to the Château de Villandry in the Loire Valley, we'd originally had in mind intensive planting of intricate patterns within the criss-crossed paths. We then realised wisely that an army of gardeners would be needed to cope

A close-run thing.

213

Previous page The western end. *Above* Stepover apples enclose the vegetable beds at the eastern end.

A blaze of colour from the wallflowers and tulips at the western end.

Fine marble figures depicting the four seasons.

The figures are shielded by hornbean niches.

Starting point for the north-facing trellis border.

with the constant planting and replanting. We opted for grass and came to appreciate the calm of the green spaces. All-over planting would have been far too 'busy'. We were unprepared for Villandry's size – twelve acres compared with our two – and the complexity of what is undoubtedly one of the world's great gardens. We returned home chastened, realising we were not in its league. We did, however, plant the west and east ends intensively. The stepover apples amongst the vegetables attract much comment.

We went on more visits abroad: to France, and one each to India and Holland. While on holiday in France we visited the magnificent chateau Vaux-le-Vicomte near Melun, fifty-five kilometres southeast of Paris. The grand garden included a temporary exhibition devoted to the work of André le Nôtre, the seventeenth century garden designer and principal gardener to Louis XIV of France, who was portrayed in the 2014 film *A Little Chaos*. We made sketches for George which led to an extensive redesign for the inside of the south wall. Originally we used *Rosa* 'Rambling Rector' and the climbers *Rosa* 'Madame Alfred Carrière' and *R.* 'Souvenir de la Malmaison' as suitable for a north-facing wall but their vigour greatly exceeded the space available and they were moved to a similar situation at the end of the stables. The less ambitious climber *Rosa* 'Madame Grégoire Staechelin' took their place.

With Simon and Sharon Hornby, we had visited the renowned garden Le Vasterival created by Princess Greta Sturdza at Sainte-Marguerite-sur-Mer in Normandy. We liked and duly mimicked her use of roses to create a thirty-nine-inch dome by training the

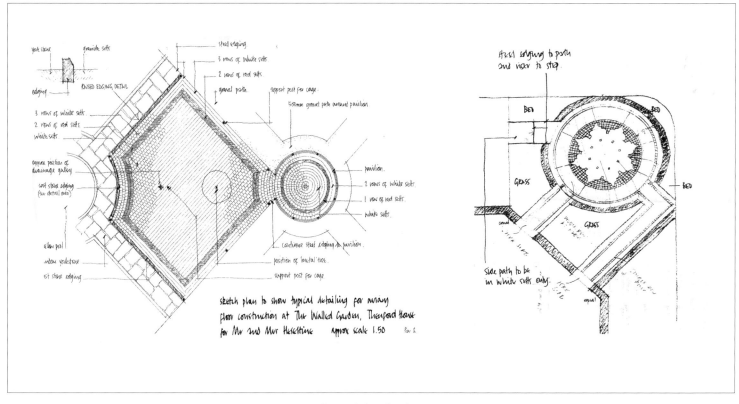

George's first sketches.

Planted up, the trellis border starts to take shape.

The yew and box topiary gives structure all-year-round.

Hybrids of *Paeonia rockii* were planted in pairs...

...with some along the trellis border.

...and others on each side of the western gate leading to the orchard.

Rosa 'Rambling Rector' trained to form a mound.

Rosa 'Rambling Rector' does well.

Lead upstand with MW initials at the north gate.

branches to form areas and pegging the ends into the ground. This encourages flowering along the branch. Yew topiary features prominently and hybrids of *Paeonia rockii* from Will McLewin of Phedar Nursery provide spectacular spring colour, underplanted by cranesbill (*Geranium himalayense*). A return visit to the flea market in Paris led us to a set of marble four seasons. These are nineteenth century, very attractive, all based on the same young girl – possibly the daughter of the unknown artist. They have been set into hornbeam buttresses alongside the east wall and its picking area.

The third visit – to India – which contributed significantly to the new Walled Garden was arranged by the Furniture History Society of which Anne was a member. It was led by Amin Jaffer who, although of Indian birth, had spent much of his life in Africa and then at a Canadian University. He had become fascinated by Indian Culture, written his first book and produced his first exhibition at the V&A Museum. He is now International Director of Asian Art at Christie's London. As a break from the tour he took some of its members to Meehra Farm, which specialised in the sale of architectural remnants, sculptures and garden ornaments, displayed in the open air or barns.

Anne fell in love with a pair of nineteenth century marble elephants some four feet high, carved as for a carnival parade with mahouts astride and garlanded with flowers. After some telephone negotiations, three months later they took their place at the Walled Garden's entrance. With the sixteen pavilions and water fountains, they contribute to the suggestion often proposed but denied by George Carter that the design of the garden is inspired by Mughal culture.

During our shopping trip to Robert Tjebbes of De Limieten nursery in Holland (described in the next chapter) we bought the *Wisteria floribunda* 'Multijuga' for the arches inside the west wall of the Walled Garden, which they share with roses and clematis.

At one point, we were much attracted by a lead upstand with Michael Wodhull's initials *MW* embossed on it. It was too much of a coincidence to resist when it appeared for sale at Christie's. We bought it for installation in the Walled Garden. Not long after, we discovered it had been stolen and had to be returned to its rightful owners, though not before we had obtained permission to make the replica that took its place inside the gate in the north wall.

Such is the story of how we designed and built this important part of our garden. Of course we would have made fewer mistakes if we had delegated even more of the work to those with experience but it would not have been such fun. It would not have been 'ours'.

Above Elephants carved in India flank the path towards 'Coanda'. *Next page* Looking across the Herb Garden.

Chapter Nine

THE HERBACEOUS BORDERS, ALLÉE & FOUNTAIN GARDEN

From your seat in a classical gazebo, your gaze is drawn through 'moon gates' in the hedge to spectacular views, while colourful borders shimmer in summer and autumn.

by Michael Heseltine

THENFORD
The Creation of an
English Garden

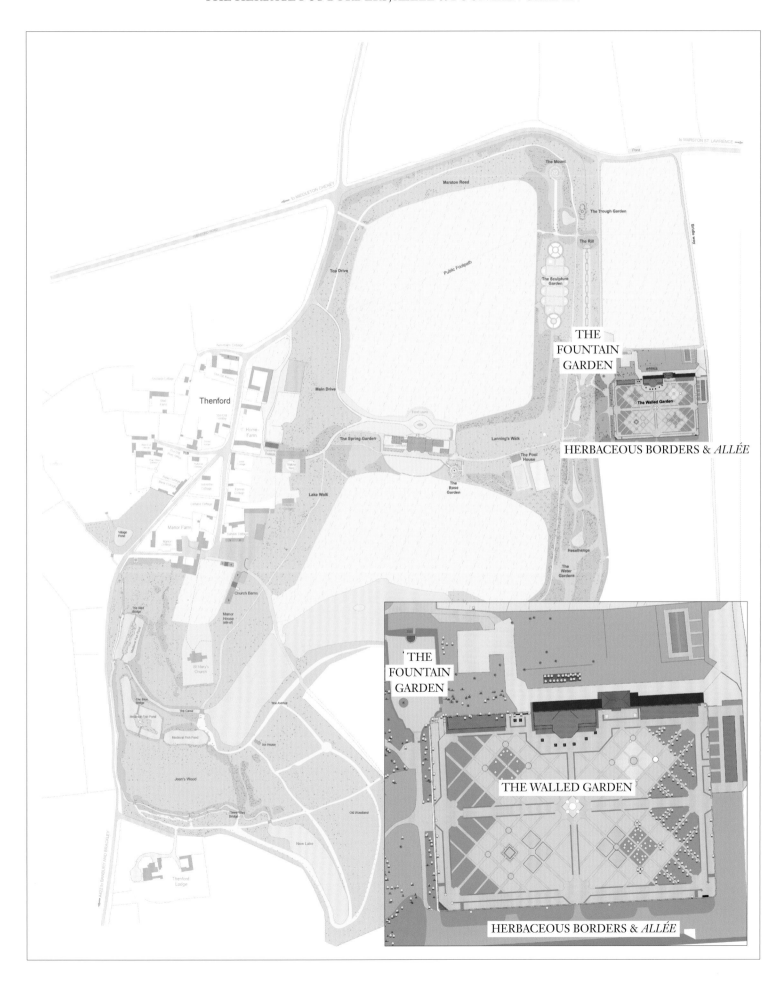

QUITE EARLY ON IN THE WORK ON the Walled Garden, Darren Webster had drawn my attention to the wooden gate securely fastened in the southern wall. He had arranged a ladder to get a view of the area beyond. It was a spectacular vista of farmland but the immediate area just outside the wall was overgrown with brambles. We remembered the *allée* at Hidcote Manor and decided to enclose a cut grass lawn within a beech hedge along the length of the south wall.

But the beech hedge would have hidden the spectacle of our farmland stretching up towards Farthinghoe, the neighbouring village, and over towards the Barnett's estate at Purston. Happily, George Carter's arrival to work on the Walled Garden coincided with the creation of the *allée* and borders, and he suggested that we incorporate two 'moon gates' – circular openings – into the hedge. We had seen a similar idea at Hidcote. We had used young beech about five to six feet high from Wyevale for the hedge so we ordered two iron circular frames and trained the plants around.

The south-facing wall outside the Walled Garden called out for

Outside the south wall before the *allée*.

Creating a 'moon gate'.

The newly-planted borders.

herbaceous borders – four of them, enclosed by curved yew buttresses topped by round clipped balls. We planned the planting carefully on paper. The two outer and the two inner beds were to be replicas of each other. And unsurprisingly, having created the south-facing summer borders, we duly decided to create autumn borders in the west-facing border in the old orchard.

George seemed to know instinctively what we wanted before we realised it ourselves. Anne mentioned *en passant* that there were magnificent baroque benches on the verandahs of Boughton House, the great Northamptonshire home of the Buccleuch family. Next time she saw George he had already been to have a look and came back with a drawing of a simplified version suitable for our gazebos. These were located against the wall opposite the two 'windows', opening onto the spectacular views over our land. Ten years later the planting had matured. Now, sitting in the gazebo on a summer evening, truly we look out over 'our peace (*sic*) of England'. George also designed seats to set into the beech hedge as viewing points for the borders.

One of the two gazebos that divide the borders to make splendid sitting places.

The borders start to come to maturity...

...and our plans come to fruition...

...with a blaze of colour...

...culminating in the autumn borders on the west side.

Previous page The gazebos align with the 'moon gates' for pleasing views. *Above* Marking out the site for the yew castle.

De Limieten pick and mix.

I mentioned four visits in our story about the Walled Garden and its surrounding areas but so far have only described three. The fourth shows just how interrelated these various projects were at the time. The purpose of this fourth visit was to choose plants for the Rill. Xa Tollemache suggested we go to see Robert Tjebbes at De Limieten, and – fully aware of her reputation as a garden designer – we suspected we were in for something special. The English horticultural industry has come on apace in supplying mature plants since then but, at the time, visiting De Limieten, which is near Amsterdam, was an event in itself. What we experienced was that of the child in the proverbial sweetshop. It was pick and mix gone mad – row upon row of trees of carefully-controlled shapes. They are moved at regular intervals to form compacted rootballs which prepares them for sale to the design and construction industries as substantial trees or sculpted shapes.

So, while we had gone to De Limieten looking for yew trees for the Rill – and chose, as well, three sixteen feet coastal redwoods (*Sequoia sempervirens*) for it – the temptation proved too much. We were shown a range of clipped yew rectangles about twelve feet high and three feet wide that in effect were a gardener's Lego kit. You could create your own concept and match the box shapes together to build it. We chose enough shapes to make a castellated square about twenty feet across for the eastern end of the *allée* outside the Walled Garden within which to display an Adam urn. At the other end we located a massive reconstituted stone urn purchased on our annual holiday near L'Isle-sur-la-Sorgue in Provence. Outside De Limieten's office there was also a box hedge. The process was the same: choose shaped box balls of different sizes, and match them together to create the image of a cloud formation.

We had completed the transformation of the Walled Garden and its hinterlands. But there were two areas yet to plan – the old orchard to the west of the Walled Garden and the gap to the northwest of it, on the land between Bridge Pond through which one had to pass on the way to the Rill.

The old orchard had originally been part of the aviary and was on the main walk to the house. To the side of the path is our remarkable ash, perhaps 200 to 300 years old. Of particular interest are the two now-champion trees – the jar fir (*Abies vejarii*) and *Quercus semecarpifolia* – that Keith Rushforth let us remove from the garden of the house he was selling in 1987. The Walled Garden's west wall alongside the orchard is now backed by the two herbaceous mixed borders, designed for autumn colour, that include *Rosa moyesii*, *moyesii* var. *fargesii*, *moyesii* f. *rosea* and the *moyesii* hybrids 'Arthur Hillier',

The castle has become the focal point of the east end of the *allée*.

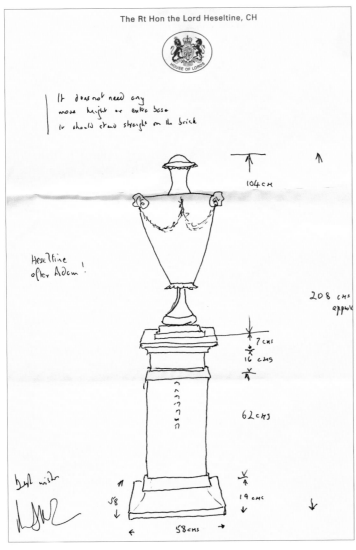

The Rt Hon the Lord Heseltine, CH

It does not need any
more height or extra base
It should stand straight on the brick

104 CM

Heseltine
after Adam!

208 cms
approx

7 cms

16 cms

62 cms

19 cms

58cms

Best wishes

Heseltine after Adam.

Urn in a junkyard.

The ancient ash's roots are impressive.

'Eddie's Jewel', 'Eos', 'Geranium' and 'Highdownensis'.

That still left the gap between the Walled Garden and the Rill. It had no feature to distinguish it. There were several self-sewn yew trees of about ten feet dotted around on land that sloped down from east to west and through which a small path to the potting sheds curved around the west and north sides of the wall. We decided to cut into the slope to flatten the area, transplant the yews into a line at the northern end and enclose the other sides in a yew hedge.

To give character to the whole, we purchased an early French wall fountain from the flea market and set it off with a cloud hedge of box. The entrance from the Walled Garden is formed by another Jim Horrobin gate, one of a pair Anne gave me for my seventieth birthday. They feature magnolia flowers from the garden. The other gate marks the entrance to the herbaceous borders to the east. An entrance leading to the Rill at the northwest corner is guarded by a pair of carved lions removed from the Houses of Parliament in the renovation of the 1930s and purchased by us from Architectural Heritage at the time we were doing the work.

The House of Commons lions.

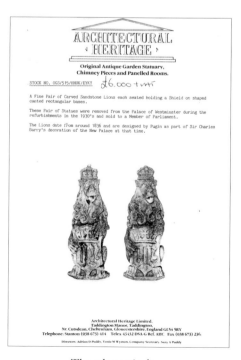

The sale particulars.

Building the Fountain Garden.

Above The French fountain sits within the cloud hedge formed from clipped box. *Next page, left* Finial on Jim Horrobin's gates to the western border and Fountain Gard

DARREN WEBSTER
Our head gardener

Darren Webster came to work as Deputy Head Gardener at Thenford in September 1996, straight from three years at the Royal Botanic Gardens, Kew.

Brought up in County Durham, and with his family roots in farming, Darren originally studied agriculture at Durham Agricultural College, Houghall. After qualifying in 1985, he worked in agriculture until 1988 when his hobby prompted a change of career and he started on his own as a jobbing gardener. He was fortunate that his uncle had a building company; as a teenager, Darren had gained significant insight into the business by helping out on projects.

In 1992, Darren decided to return to Houghall College to gain a formal horticulture qualification. He obtained his National Certificate in Horticulture with distinction a year later. He collected the award for the best NCH student and best practical student as well as the Northumbria in Bloom Ellis Wood Award for best student gardener of 1993.

On the advice of his lecturers, Darren applied for the three-year Kew Diploma in Horticulture Course in September 1993. While at Kew he participated in two botanical expeditions to Lesotho in 1994 and late 1995 to the Drakensberg Mountains in Lesotho and Natal, after winning the Stanley Smith Travel Fund Scholarship.

In September 1996 he graduated with honours and also won the Matilda Smith Memorial Prize for best practical student. He gained other awards: the G. C. Johnson Memorial Prize for best overall performance on the Kew Diploma Course and the Tony Kirkham Arboricultural Prize. He was President of the Student Union during his last year.

It was a stroke of good fortune that brought him to Thenford. As the end of his course approached, he had begun conversations to take up a job with The Royal Parks. However, economic conditions had led to a freeze on public sector recruitment and the competitive processes for such jobs added further uncertainty. A colleague of Darren's had applied for the vacancy we had. But he accepted an offer from Arabella Lennox-Boyd so he recommended our position to Darren. Twenty years later, having brought with him his far-ranging experience and exemplary qualifications, Darren has played a central role in the establishment and development of our garden. He became Head Gardener on 24 December 1997.

Chapter Ten

THE RILL

The Rill attracts much attention… the visual impact, the magic of the glittering sparkle, the splash and gurgle, the drama of shape and sound, are indispensable.

by Michael Heseltine

THENFORD
The Creation of an
English Garden

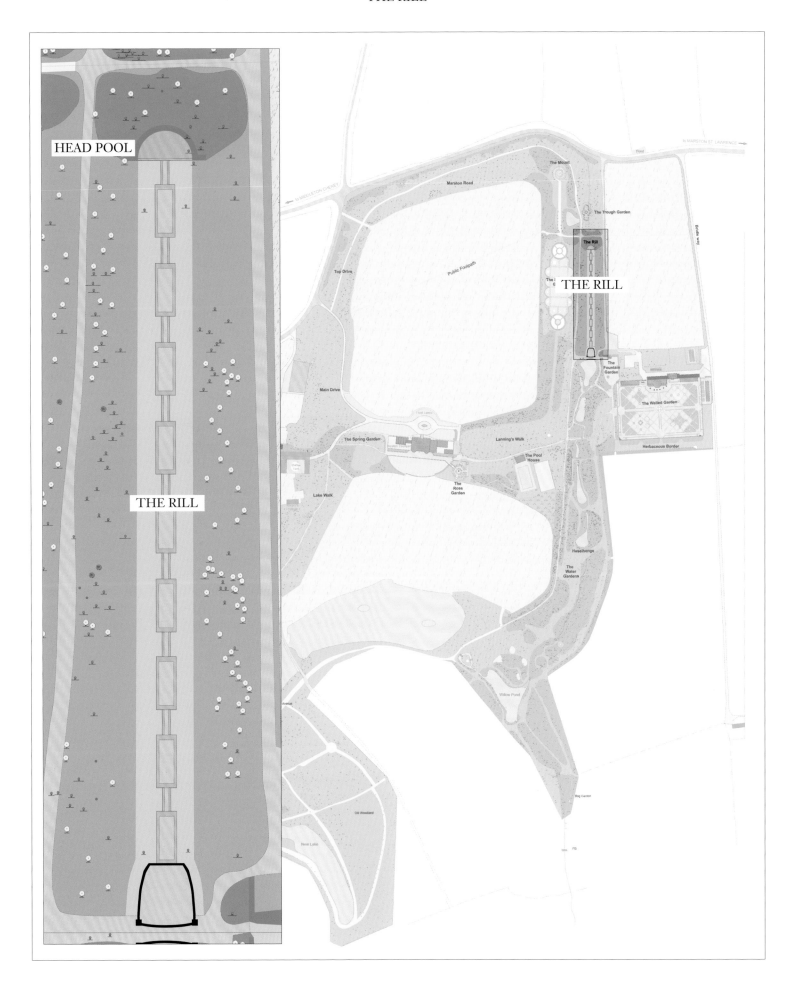

HEAD POOL

THE RILL

THE RILL

IT IS EASY TO REMEMBER WHY a long water feature seemed right for the area where the Rill now flows. It follows the line of our north-to-south stream, Marston Brook, which we talked about at length in Chapter Five: The Water Gardens. To recap briefly, the stream ran through a rectangular space about 700 feet long by 180 feet wide, bordered to the east by a field and to the west by the path that curves right round the north of the arboretum. Our plantings of two straight shelter belts of deciduous trees, conifers and yews followed the long edges of this rectangle. The brook, set in a deep ditch and overgrown with nettles and brambles, was a nightmare to maintain. Viewed from the southern end, there was an obvious opportunity for a structured approach.

How or where we got the idea to build a rill is uncertain. We had visited some of the great gardens of Italy and seen their majestic use of water. By this time, George Carter had begun work on the Walled Garden and we asked him to come up with some suggestions. Later, George produced evidence to support my claim to parenthood. I had sketched an idea for a rill and sent George a page torn from a newspaper colour supplement showing a finished project in Canada. He

One of George Carter's proposals.

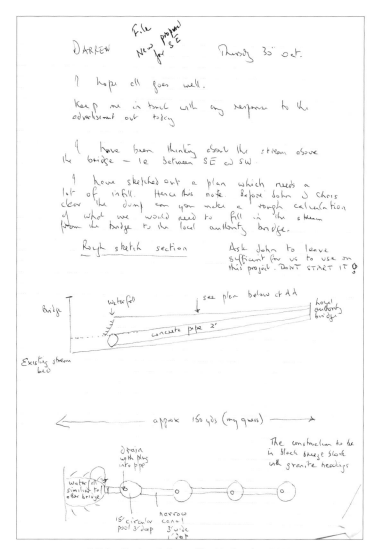

Michael's sketch for a rill - 30 October 2001

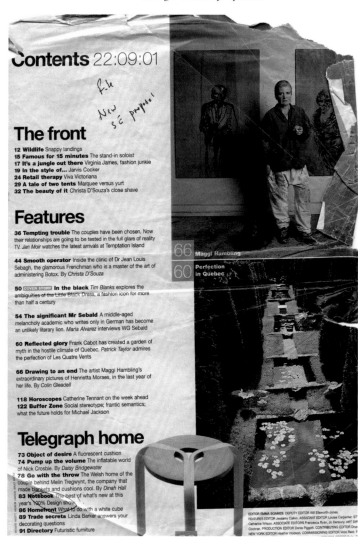

Cutting from the *Daily Telegraph* - 22 September 2001.

Another of George's schemes.

PLATFORM Nº 3

RUSTIC PAVILION ON RUSTIC BRIDGE
WITH FLINT OBELISK IN A GLADE

PLAN OF PLATFORM & PAVILION

He explored this too...

...and looked at this option.

Where the Rill would be constructed.

Marston Brook's original channel...

...the local authority bridge that crossed it.

We channeled it into this three-foot pipe...

submitted a number of options but we asked him to work up a project based on the original concept. Certainly, out of all this came a clear decision and George went to work on the drawings.

Achieving the greatest visual impact needed the longest perspective. To get that, we needed to move the public right of way that ran across the north of the area. After proper consultation, we had little difficulty in securing approval. That left the ditch – and, luckily, there was an obvious solution. We cleared its banks, buried a three-foot diameter pipe to carry the stream, and levelled the surface. With the removal of a handful of large trees, we had a spectacular, tree-lined, gently sloping site.

We had also removed the need for the local authority bridge over the right of way. Our plan included the rebuilding of the stone bridge at the south end, incorporating the old headstone we'd found in the courtyard of the house. It is dated 1580 and its Latin inscription '1580 anno Domini DOMUS PROPRIA, DOMUS OPTIMA EST' translates as *Year of the Lord 1580 One's own house is the best house.* Sadly, the origin of this little tag is unknown. It is assumed that it was taken from the original mediaeval/tudor house. But the initials underneath are unexplained. They are 'N A E T' and are arranged in a square. Anne consulted Dr Howard Colvin, the Architectural Historian of St John's College, Oxford, but sadly he could not solve the puzzle either.

The Rill starts with a curved headpool then, flowing south, there are nine rectangular pools each about thirty feet long and ten feet wide, with interconnecting channels fifteen feet long. Each pool has four fountains and the whole depends on a complex pumping system fed from Bridge Pond at the top of the Water Gardens. The gentle slope of the site helps create a gravity flow. As well as having the help of George Carter and Roger Balmer, the project we began in August 2002 needed the services of a structural engineer, a water engineer, an irrigation specialist and an electrician.

The nine linked pools with their inter-connecting channels are

...and landscaped over it.

identical. But the head pool is very different. We were staying with Mark and Arabella Lennox-Boyd when they showed us a feature in their rose garden by Maggy Howarth. We knew at once that we wanted to commission Maggy to design our headpool. She inspected the site and submitted a design. Simply described, she proposed a scallop shell with an intricate pattern of coloured pebbles, seashells and brightly coloured quartzes. A shallow covering of water enhances these colours. It is edged with stone into which we incorporated my initials and the date. A few of our pebbles were hand-picked on Scottish beaches – something that would now be prohibited but in Asia there are no restrictions and there are dealers in these river stones. Most of ours came from Nanjing Province in China or, to a lesser extent, Surabaya, Indonesia.

We screened the northern end of the Rill with yew enclosing an Italian stone bench from Architectural Heritage. Alongside the fountains we planted sculpted yew trees from De Limieten, who supplied three men to help us plant them. At the southern end the water

Form-work filled with concrete.

One of the nine pools takes shape.

The ninth pool at the southern end.

Finally, the pumping station down at Bridge Pond.

flows out of the last pool, cascading into a rockery created with large stones from the estate. In late summer the giant cowslips (*Primula florindae*) provide a tableau of yellow against the sheet of tumbling water. To complete the setting, we bought three coastal redwoods and three large Japanese maples, again from De Limieten. We could have bought small trees but we decided to create a more immediate impact and chose these trees for the purpose.

Between the Rill and the top of the Water Gardens a secondary access to the Walled Garden crossed the brook over a stone and corrugated sheeting bridge. We invited George to design a replacement which would be capable of bearing the load of the much larger horticultural equipment now used in the arboretum. This allowed us to divert the machinery away from the more ornate eighteenth century bridge lower down the stream. It was built in concrete with stone facing recycled from derelict walls and buildings. We used the cappings from one of the old greenhouses to finish each side of the bridge.

One of nine balance tanks.

The builders built a shelter in winter.

One of the nine sets of valves.

The headpool's scallop base ready to go to Thenford.

All set for its new location.

The east bank of the Rill was redesigned using more large stones from our land to create a rockery. In 2001 we commissioned Simon Allison from Cropredy, Oxfordshire, to make a fountain for Bridge Pond. It is inspired by four leaves we chose from the spectacular *Gunnera* at Gunnera Pond. From them, Simon cast life-size bronze replicas to create the fountain.

The Rill is now so dominant a feature that it is easy to forget the trees that border it. Amongst the conifers are the bristlecone pine (*Pinus aristata*), the purple-coned spruce (*Picea purpurea*), *Abies fraseri* and the blue Douglas fir (*Pseudotsuga menziesii* var. *glauca*). There is a curious lime (*Tilia sp.*) with a HERS 2808 collection number which is still to be identified. We are told there is only one other known. The Japanese snowbell (*Styrax japonicus*) is a dainty, small tree and the *Magnolia* 'Black Tulip' is one of our favourites. The double-flowered *Prunus avium* 'Plena' is glorious in the spring

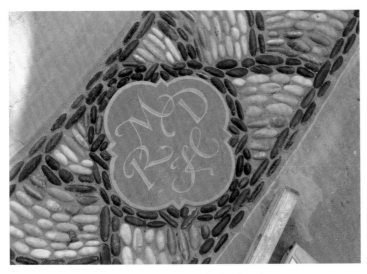

Michael's initials on the headpool.

The date of the headpool.

The Italian stone bench above the pool.

De Limieten's trees arrive.

Pouring the fountain pool for the mosaic base.

The Rill begins to take shape.

The bridge ready for its stone-facing...

...and with its 1580 headstone in place.

The bridge, pipe and pumping station.

The Rill nearly finished, viewed from the north.

while the elder (*Sambucus nigra* f. *porphyrophylla* 'Gerda') cries out for a pink-flowered clematis to climb through it.

When all the work was finished, the result was everything we had hoped for – to start with! It wasn't long before we noticed a sickliness in the yews. We'd forgotten about the clay underlining our soil. Using heavy earth-moving equipment up and down the site had meant that we had effectively planted the yews in clay-lined buckets. Yews will not tolerate that amount of water. Fortunately, there was an easy solution: we laid a small drain to carry the surplus water away from the planting pockets into the buried stream.

We've never found a satisfactory way to keep the Rill clean. From Bridge Pond, all the water needed has to be pumped in nine separate circuits. They, in their turn, supply the thirty-six fountain jets. The result is indeed spectacular but far from maintenance-free. The easiest answer would be to keep the system running full-time. The individual pools are deep enough if a constant flow of water

Left The ninth pool. *Above* The gunnera fountain being placed.

It sits beside the new rockery in Bridge Pond.

The rockery on the bridge's north side.

Yew cones from de Limieten and stones for rockery.

inhibits algae growth. But the cost would be prohibitive. So, when it is warm we are faced with the problem of removing a mass of blanket weed by hand. The nozzles of the jets trap leaves and the inevitable detritus, and the multiplicity of pumps frequently need our plumber's call-out service.

The Rill attracts much attention at any time of the year. It is a central part of the water features that add so much to our garden. Without them, it would be a dull old place. Certainly there are problems and no little cost, but the magic of the glittering sparkle, the splash and gurgle, the pure drama of shape and sound, are an indispensable part of the achievement. And, if you were to look on the really bright side, the late Duke of Marlborough told me shortly before he died that he faced a bill of £1m to restore Capability Brown's magnificent lake at Blenheim.

Distinctive cones of *Abies fraseri*...

Picea purpurea...

...and *Pinus aristata*.

Pinus aristata with new growth.

...boasts vivid cones.

Styrax japonicus.

Blue Douglas fir...

...and its cone.

Styrax japonicus flowers.

Magnolia Black Tulip ('Jurmag1').

Sambucus nigra f. *porphyrophylla* 'Gerda'

Chapter Eleven

THE ROSE GARDEN

White roses predominate in a thoughtfully restructured garden rescued from mediocrity,

where 100 different snowdrops also flourish – and two cherubs have a tale to tell.

by Anne Heseltine

THENFORD
The Creation of an
English Garden

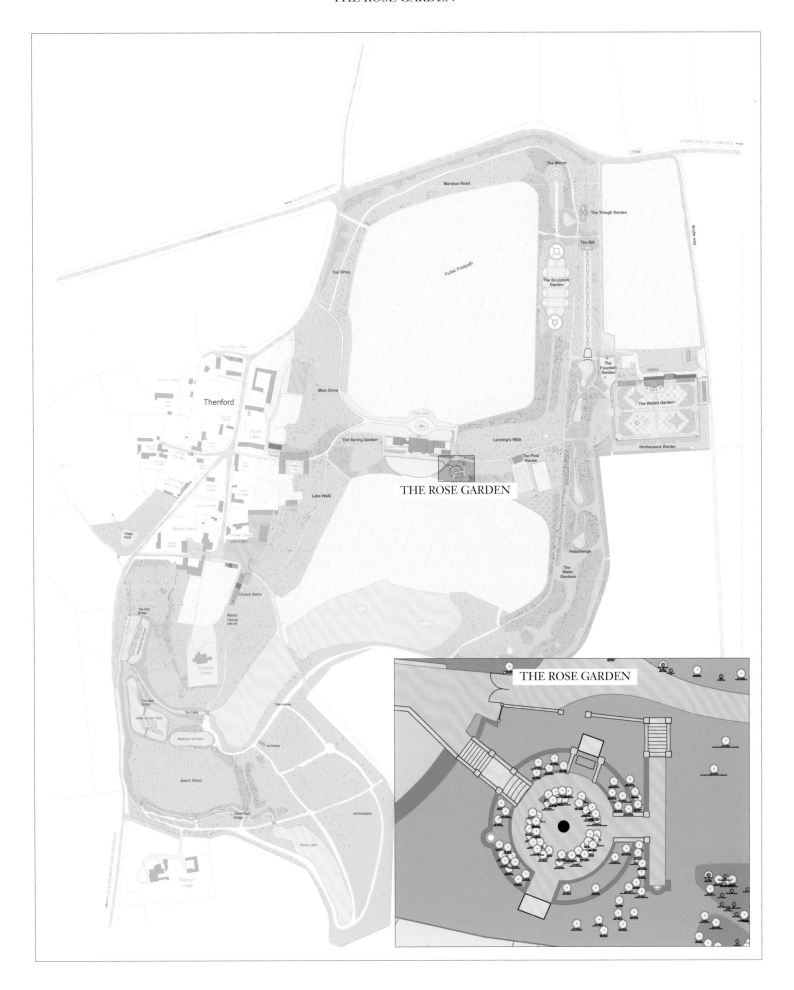

THE ROSE GARDEN

THE ROSE GARDEN

IN JUNE 2003 WE CELEBRATED our garden's developments with a large lunch to which many members of the professional, commercial and social world of horticulture were invited. George Carter and Roger Balmer's work on the herbaceous borders, the Walled Garden, the Fountain Garden and the Rill had all evolved in a sequence governed by their proximity. There was one area near the house that had rather been left behind and to which we then directed our attention.

Long before we arrived, there had been a rose garden just alongside the south lawn. It was roughly circular and presented the particular design challenge of combining two unrelated axes. The first was a series of wider steps leading down from the lawn. The other was a grass walk heading off at an angle between cotoneaster hedging to the east. Early in our time, the then Head Gardener, Andrew Peters, advised by Lanning Roper, had got rid of this hedge and created the Long Border leading to the pool and tennis court. The steps down were adequate but had been amateurishly built. They lacked the precision demanded by the formality of the concept that we had in mind. There was then another level of rose beds retained by rough stone walling through which more steps in a gap led to the Long Border.

George's design followed the original basic concept although the execution was of an altogether different standard. He proposed the same two entrances: the steps down from the lawn and a new flight of stone steps cut into the bank from the main path leading to the

George Carter's concept sketches...

...showed how the Rose Garden could be transformed.

264

Two flights of steps in the old rose garden.

Old planting removed ready for the new design.

Marking out the foundations...

...where the steps will rise.

A pair of massive stone pillars at the entrance.

The arbour completed.

The new flight of steps down from the courtyard.

The first planting goes in.

Looking down from the South Lawn to the new layout.

Walled Garden. The second approach was dramatically enhanced by yew niches containing marble statues and a pair of massive stone pillars. The building plans were interpreted with white paint on the ground. The completed stonework followed.

In 2007 Robert Mattock (see also Chapter Thirteen) drew a planting sketch for my choice of mostly white roses for the outer beds. As well as *Rosa × alba* 'Alba Semiplena', with its greyish-green leaves, and fragrant *Rosa rugosa* 'Alba', I selected the highly fragrant pure white 'Blanche Double de Coubert' and 'Dupontii', which has a large boss of golden stamens. Also on my list were sweetly scented, repeat-flowering 'Fimbriata' and the unscented but outstandingly pure white 'Frau Karl Druschki'. I chose 'Frühlingsgold' for its very fragrant, light golden-yellow flowers, 'Maiden's Blush' for its greyish-green foliage and fragrant, double, pale pinkish-cream flowers, and 'Nevada' which has scented, creamy-white, semi-double flowers. Last but not least were 'Prosperity', notable for its large clusters of creamy-white, double flowers, and soft pink, highly-scented 'Souvenir de Saint Anne's', along with cream Tynwald ('Mattwyt') and White Cloud ('Korstacha'), which has fragrant double white flowers tinged cream at the middle. The centre beds have standard *Rosa* Swany ('Meiburenac') which were originally underplanted with *Rosa* 'White

Pet', Lanning Roper's favourite. Rabbits did great damage, particularly to the four inner beds which in early 2016 were replanted with the low-growing *Rosa* Flower Carpet White ('Noaschnee').

George's design included a pretty stone-backed arbour – under ten feet high and covered by a climbing *Rosa* 'Madame Alfred Carrière' – in which we were able to set a substantial oak bench that has our initials *M* and *A* intricately entwined on its back. Arabella Lennox-Boyd had designed the original for her husband, with *M* standing for Mark. As soon as we saw it, the coincidence with our initials was irresistible. We were delighted that Arabella was happy to make another version for us. A large yew on the bank behind has the rambler *Rosa* 'Seagull' set to clamber through it.

The Rose Garden's centrepiece is a Venetian well-head. When we bought it, its superstructure was modern and out of sympathy with the original stone base. Victor and Annamaria Edelstein, friends who lived in Venice, photographed a period well near their home that enabled us to commission Jim Horrobin to craft an ironwork replica.

The Rose Garden's first ornaments – a pair of jolly eighteenth century lead cherubs toasting each other from pillars on opposite sides of the steps – have a tale to tell. They were stolen at night, and we were very sad to lose them. Not long after, two nice old lead urns

The stone arbour with *Rosa* 'Madame Alfred Carrière'.

Arabella Lennox-Boyd's seat.

269

were also stolen from outside our front door in the middle of the day.

Our anger was much tempered because the theft of the cherubs had a happy ending. Our daughter Alexandra was staying with friends in Shropshire. The weather was wet so they decided to go to Ludlow to visit antique shops. In the window of one were our cherubs! She went inside and said to the shop owner how attractive they were. He agreed enthusiastically and, much to her surprise, told her they came from an old house in the Midlands that was about to become a convent. 'I bought them the other day at a local auction,' the dealer said.

It all sounded highly unlikely and Alexandra left the shop to rejoin her friends in the car outside. So keen was the dealer to show off his new wares that he hadn't cleaned them up. White bird lime was smeared across the head of one of the cherubs. Alexandra telephoned us from the car, and Michael told the local Banbury police to whom we had already reported the loss. They contacted Ludlow police who knew the local auction house well and sent a constable around to find out how they'd obtained them. It transpired that the cherubs had been brought in by 'a chap we know well – he always brings us in good things!' Because the auctioneers dealt with him so often they always paid him cash rather than make him wait for payment for several weeks, as most auction houses do. Of course, when his address and telephone number were checked they were bogus. Our case was quickly proven: a weekend guest had sent us some photographs taken just before the theft that showed the cherubs with their identifying smear of bird lime. By the following Tuesday the cherubs were back in the Rose Garden. We'd been taught serious lessons about security.

There are three yew niches in the Rose Garden. Two are already filled while the third awaits an appropriate companion. Both sculptures, which we bought from Summers Place Auctions in Billingshurst,

Rosa 'Wedding Day'.

Rosa 'White pet'.

Left The Venetian well head by Jim Horrobin. *Above* lead cherubs (18th c).

Pan playing his pipes among *Rosa* 'White Pet'.

The cure for this untidy corner...

...was the curved stone ericaceous bed...

...which we overplanted! *Right* A bronze raven by Dido Crosby.

Great white cherry (*Prunus* 'Tai-haku').

Sussex, are white marble and depict characters from classical mythology – a Centaur, and a Pan playing his pipes. Initially the idea was to obtain plinths in the same material but the cost frightened us. As a temporary measure, we decided to mount them on concrete blocks – then, on a visit to the Yorkshire Sculpture Park, near Wakefield, we noticed that they had used these blocks too. Theirs had weathered well and looked perfectly acceptable. Our blocks are there to stay.

The close proximity of a raven on one of the stone columns can worry visitors. There is no need to fret: it is Dido Crosby's remarkable bronze sculpture, a particularly agreeable present for one birthday. We thought the raven might see off other birds. No such luck! Birds see him as a convenient perch and he is usually covered in lime. We were particularly pleased to add Dido's raven to her goat in the Sculpture Garden. We had first met her as a child at our London home in Chepstow Villas when she visited with her father Theo, the architect, writer and sculptor whom we knew from the early days of Haymarket.

It is obvious that a rose garden is about roses. In ours, there are a few exceptions. The great white cherry (*Prunus* 'Tai-haku) came with the initial Hillier order and for a brief few weeks each spring dominates the view of the lake and countryside from Arabella's seat. The *Clematis* 'Jackmanii Alba' is set to conquer one of the two columns. People say *Ilex perado* subsp. *platyphylla* from the Canary Islands needs protection and preferably a south-facing wall. That is what we have at the back of the Rose Garden and it seems to have been appreciated. But there's a mistake looming in the form of the Californian scrub oak (*Quercus berberidifolia*). In its early days, with its tiny leaves, it had all the characteristics of a medium shrub. Against the same retaining wall in full sun, it has taken off and is heading who-knows-where.

We use the rose beds as a nursery for about 100 different snowdrops. This brings the great advantage of a well-defined location with hard paths near the house that creates interest early in the year. Single, or at most three, relatively expensive bulbs start their life with us here until, after a few years, there are enough for us to transfer to more remote locations.

Some years before we redesigned the Rose Garden itself, there was an untidy corner between it and the house. We invited Carolyn Cumming, who had designed the garden around the pool and Summer House, to come up with a scheme. The corner was in the shade and it seemed sensible to buy in ericaceous soil so we could grow acid-loving plants. We adopted Carolyn's proposal for a curved stone bed and planted mostly camellias, magnolias and a Japanese *Rhododendron yakushimanum* given to us by Ted and Carol Hughes. Our mistake was to over-plant and we had to start again some ten years later.

Anyone who undertakes change in the structure of a garden faces the dilemma of cost. The temptation to cut expenditure, do it yourself and hope for the best is ever present. We did not change the concept of the Rose Garden significantly but its new structures and the quality of the workmanship were transformational. Our Rose Garden will now last for generations to come.

Chapter Twelve

THE TROUGH GARDEN

A trick of the mind inspires a unique garden where wisteria, rhododendrons, alpine
perennials and rare species provide year-round interest and immense pleasure.

by Michael Heseltine

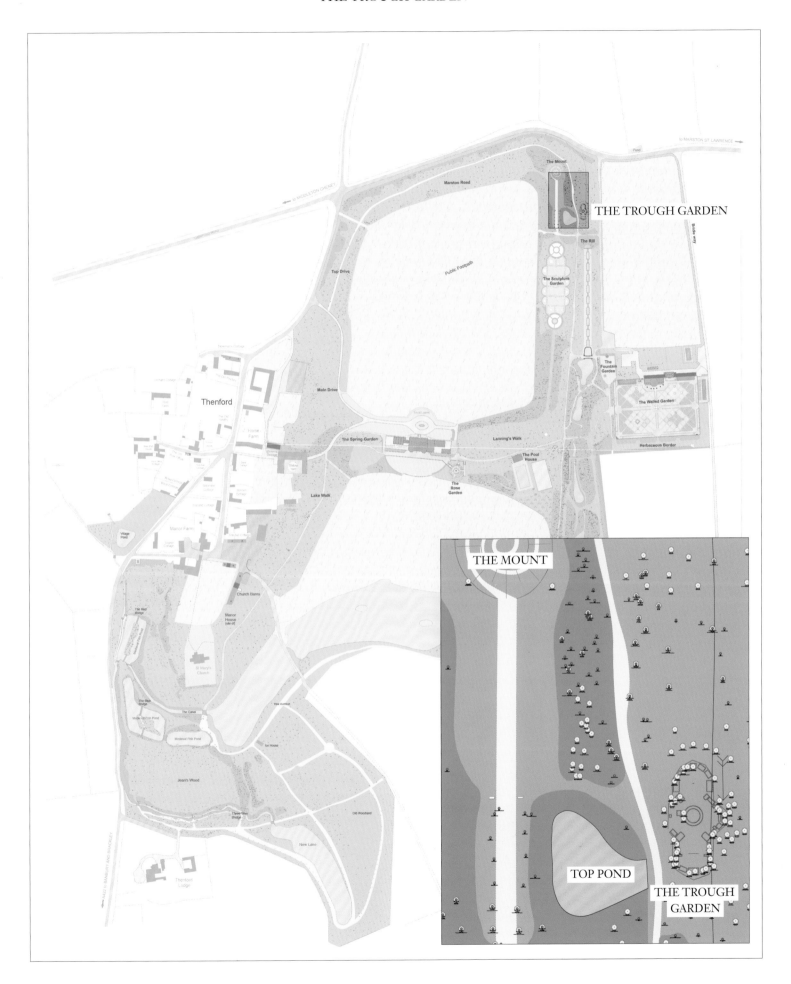

THE TROUGH GARDEN

THE MOUNT

TOP POND

THE TROUGH GARDEN

OVER THE YEARS WE HAVE often stayed with Richard and Mary Carew Pole at Antony in Cornwall. As a National Trust property, it is much admired by visitors both for its architecture and the quality of its garden. I had an inspirational memory from one of our visits that remained tucked away in a corner of my mind – a standard wisteria growing in a granite trough quite close to the house. The memory never faded and provoked the idea of a garden of troughs which, from time to time, I mentioned to Anne as a project we should develop.

At the RHS Hampton Court Palace Flower Show in 2009 we passed a small stall owned by Julia Skinner whose family-run business – J's Garden Antiques – sells historic architectural items. She had seven different sized troughs for sale. We moved on but a few moments later Anne said: 'You've always talked about it. This is as good a time as any. Get on with it'. We bought five.

Before the arrival of pumped water systems and metal tanks, stone troughs were used as drinking bowls for cattle or sheep on Britain's farms. They came in every size and shape and are now frequently used as garden planters once drainage holes have been bored through the bottom. With patience, over some eighteen months we collected thirty-eight and, as they arrived, lined them up outside the potting sheds. We tracked them down in a variety of obvious ways. The Internet led us to some in scrap yards, we found others through our earlier contacts with Architectural Heritage and Summers Place Auctions, while a friend of our son-in-law, Nick Williams, was disposing of one of the biggest troughs. The greatest boost was delivered by Carol Hughes whom I sat next to at dinner while staying with Simon and Hilary Day in Devon. She told me of a dealer, Ben Jones, in Moretonhampstead, North Devon, who had not been well and had a considerable stock. I asked Darren Webster to explore what was on offer. He rang me, excited not just by the numbers but by the opportunity to acquire a granite cider press. It is a circular trough carved from granite around which a pony or donkey would have pulled a large, circular, flat-edged stone wheel to squeeze the juice from the apples into the trough's well. It is now the centrepiece of our Trough Garden and, with a bit of imagination, gives the impression of a work by Barbara Hepworth. In all, we added ten troughs to the collection that day.

North of the Rill and to the east of the Top Pond there remained one of the two open spaces left in the arboretum. This site suited our purpose particularly well because it had close access to a mains water supply. It was also reasonably flat but it was important to ensure the area was well prepared to prevent sinkage under the weight of the troughs which might upset the design. John Atkinson undertook the construction work in spring 2011, laying a base of hardcore ironstone topped by thirteen bulk bags of the same pink granite from Gravelmaster that Anne had chosen for the Sculpture Garden.

I sketched out a design for the layout of the troughs which I sent to George Carter, who returned a rather different and much better proposal. Using heavy farm lifting equipment, we took immense trouble to get the levels right: the eye would quickly detect any variation in the troughs' tops. Matching the levels was not as easy as it might appear because many of the bottoms of the troughs were rough-hewn.

Newly-bought troughs lined up near potting sheds...

...after arriving from Moretonhampstead.

The planting at Antony that created the idea.

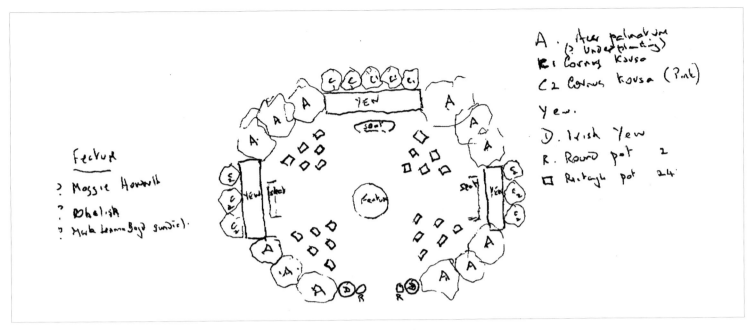

Michael's sketch plan.

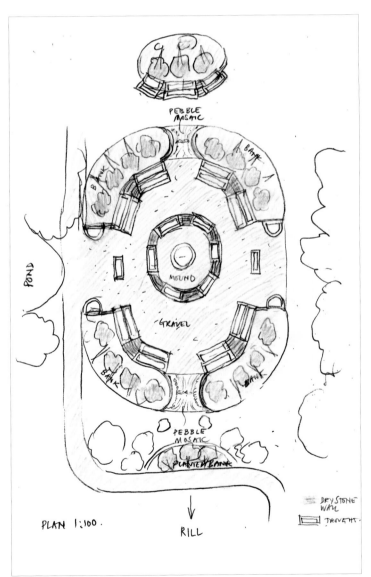

George Carter's first response.

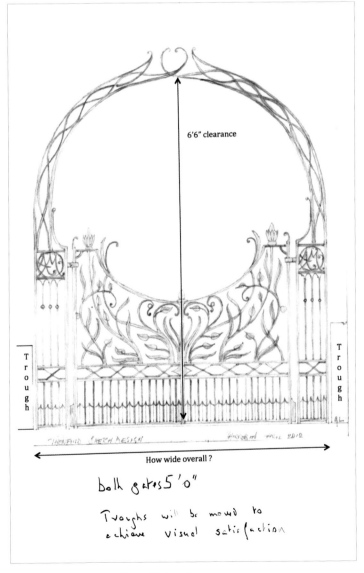

Jim Horrobin's design for the gates.

Jim Horrobin and his creation.

John Atkinson preparing the site.

We positioned the cider press centrally and filled both its trough and empty middle with soil. Then at its centre we stood a wooden pillar that we had bought at Chatsworth many years before but for which we had never found a permanent home. We placed a pair of Coalbrookdale seats on York stone paving facing inwards to the centre and built a rabbit-proof fence around the outside. The outstanding feature of the Trough Garden is the pair of gates, again designed by Jim Horrobin, which Anne gave me to celebrate our Golden Wedding anniversary in 2012. We had originally intended to plant golden roses to climb through them but decided that would obscure the design.

For two reasons, I wanted to plant an enclosing hedge. First, it would provide shelter for the plants and, second, it would preserve an element of surprise. Instead of first glimpsing the troughs from a distance, a visitor would only see the garden's full impact once inside the hedge. Perhaps I was influenced by a chance remark of Anne's that it looked a bit like a cemetery. Even if it did, it was too late to do anything about it. Whatever the reason, the clipped yew hedge does ensure privacy and shelter. Groups of *Cornus kousa* var. *chinensis* 'Wisley Queen' and *Cornus kousa* var. *chinensis* 'White Fountain' overhang it at either end. Ten *Acer palmatum* cultivars – 'Bloodgood', 'Jiro-shidare', 'Ki-hachijo', 'Killarney', 'Matsu-ga-e', 'Momenshide', 'Oridono-nishiki', 'Sango-kaku', 'Volubile' and 'Wilson's Pink Dwarf' – are planted to the front and rear for their spring foliage and autumn colour. We obtained the biggest plants we could find to help create the surprise effect we were seeking.

When we were ready to plant, each trough had to be checked to ensure it had enough drainage holes. We added three inches of large gravel to facilitate drainage. There were then other choices: neutral, alkaline or acidic soil – I love the genus *Gentiana*; full sun or full shade provided by overhanging the *Acer palmatum*; or part shade. But first there was the wisteria of my original inspiration. On my way back from a Regional Growth Fund roadshow in Margate in May 2011, I visited the National Collection of wisterias created by Chris Lane. I chose eight plants including *Wisteria brachybotrys* 'Showa-beni', *floribunda* 'Alba', *floribunda* 'Beni-fuji', *floribunda* 'Rosea', *floribunda* 'Royal Purple', *sinensis* 'Amethyst' and × *formosa*. Four are in the cider press, three in large troughs and one in a circular bed outside the gates.

For the detail of the remaining planting, we faced the familiar dilemmas we had encountered time and again over the years. While the troughs meant we could select varieties suitable for small containers and were an excellent home for alpine plants, I had never gained experience of an alpine garden and the time needed to visit some was not available, even though I know that the more one can bring personal knowledge to the selection of plants in a garden, the more it will reflect one's own preferences. So we were fortunate to enlist Stella and David Rankin of Kevock Garden Plants in Midlothian, Scotland, to help us decide what to plant and where.

We talked earlier about our initial attempts to grow rhododendrons. With the ability to choose our soil, we took the opportunity to collect very small species. Of the thirty-three different ones now in

Gentiana sino-ornata.

Gentiana 'Blue Silk'.

Gentiana × *macaulayi* 'King Fisher'.

the Trough Garden, twenty-one were obtained for us by the Rankins; a further five were given to us for our Golden Wedding by Michael and Christina Mates and Michael and Gail Jopling (Lord and Lady Jopling); and the last one by Michael and Jillian Agg of Choice Landscapes. We added seven small varieties of the Japanese maple *Acer palmatum* – 'Beni-maiko', 'Toyama-nishiki', 'Koto-ito-komachi', 'Koto-no-ito', 'Dissectum Variegatum', 'Red Pygmy' and 'Tamukeyama'. We selected them carefully for their tiny size and interspersed them with a range of dwarf fir, pine and spruce, together with a Chinese dwarf mountain ash (*Sorbus reducta*), a leather oak (*Quercus durata*) and a freak chestnut (*Aesculus hippocastanum* 'Monstrosa') that grows a matter of centimetres a year.

At the other end of the planting scale, into the troughs went a wide range of bulbs and corms – *Allium, Cyclamen, Fritillaria*, snowdrops, daffodils and tulips, many rare and from wild-collected sources. Alpine perennials fill the remaining space to provide year-round interest and great pleasure. The Rankins involved Edrom Nurseries at Coldingham, near Berwick-upon-Tweed, in their recommendations and it is from them that the three show-stopper hardy orchids (*Cypripedium flavum, C. kentuckiense* and *C. reginae*) came. We had tried this genus earlier in other parts of the garden but without success. The trough conditions were exactly what they needed and they responded

well, in one case so significantly that we have the beginnings of a colony elsewhere. The troughs containing acidic soil enabled us to plant nineteen different gentians. Not all survived but the success of others is reward enough.

We have placed hundreds of different plants in the troughs and there is an urgent need for an audit to establish those that have survived. I now read the excellent magazines of the Alpine Garden Society and The Cyclamen Society. I will certainly revisit Pottertons Nursery in Lincolnshire as I extend my search for new introductions.

A small number of plants proved invasive in the near-perfect conditions. The creeping dogwood (*Cornus canadensis*) loves the acidic soil, produces pretty white flowers and deep red autumn colour but it runs everywhere. The *Sisyrinchium idahoense* var. *macounii* seeds all over the place and is best avoided.

The areas between the troughs are in heavy shade and are often damp. Many ferns love these conditions and their foliage adds a charming setting to the austere granite of the troughs as well as a contrast to the pink of the chippings.

In order to keep track of our cataloguing, we decided to obtain labels to attach to each trough. We were on holiday in Sicily and on one of those lazy evening strolls came across a shop selling numbered ceramic labels. We placed an order from one to thirty-eight. We should

Above and right Cypripedium kentuckiense flourish in the troughs.

have anticipated the mistake because they were not able to withstand the English winter. The glaze cracked and the labels split. We found replacements in Welsh slate at a stand at the Blenheim Palace Horse Trials. They look a great deal better but even they proved controversial. Andrew Lawson, whose photographs appear extensively in this book, took many of the Trough Garden. He never said anything, but when the photographs arrived he had instructed his technician to offer us a choice with and without the labels!

Understandably, we are still offered troughs by suppliers from whom we purchased the original thirty-eight. The temptation to buy more is sometimes irresistible. I mentioned the small circular one outside the gates. It has now been joined by the largest one we have acquired and another low, long, thin one is intended to lie at the feet of another big one inside the gates. This has got to stop but we have yet to hear of anyone else who has a trough garden at all.

One final story is about a very recent trip to Antony, from where my original inspiration came. I went to visit the wisteria in its trough. However, when I arrived there, I found it didn't exist. I had assumed a wisteria some way behind the trough had actually been growing in the trough itself. It was a trick of my memory.

Frost-damaged Sicilian labels.

Left Wisteria surrounding the central pillar. *Above* The replacement labels we fitted later.

Above Stone chippings contrast with the weathered troughs. *Next page* Jim's gates are perfect.

Chapter Thirteen

COLLECTING

So far, we have named and numbered 5000 plants. We have planted 400 different

roses, 370 oaks, 350 cotoneasters, 342 snowdrops, 55 box… and much more.

by Michael Heseltine

THENFORD
The Creation of an
English Garden

AS OUR COLLECTION – FROM ALL ITS different sources – grew, it became increasingly difficult to know what would appear on our 'to plant' lists every autumn. We create them each September by combing through the nursery standing beds and selecting candidates that look man enough to face adulthood in the arboretum. That is easy to do but time-consuming to execute. Which plants will be on the standing beds, and where they will have come from a year or two earlier, is not predictable. Their source may have been seeds, gifts, cuttings or nursery purchases. It may all sound a bit amateurish but it's the way we do it. Behind this apparent jumble of decision making sit detailed computer records – but making the right individual choice can only be done reliably by looking through the nursery beds to assess the plants themselves.

Over the almost forty years we've been building the collection there have been a number of 'accelerations' to our haphazard proce-

dure. Because collecting plants is not a competitive 'I've-got-more-than-you-process', we have been constantly overwhelmed and gratified by the generosity of our horticultural friends. In Chapter Three we talked about the circumstances that led to our first purchase from Hillier and Keith Rushforth's gift of a notable variety of conifers. We have been given significant numbers of surplus plants by the Royal Botanic Gardens, Kew, the Savill Garden, Royal Botanic Garden Edinburgh and Bedgebury National Pinetum and Forest. Other happy memories include Richard and Mary Carew Pole's offer to choose whatever we wanted from the National Collection of *Hemerocallis* at Antony. Val Anderson, the head gardener, sent the first twenty-five in 1997 and followed up with another twenty-five in 1999. We are delighted that the offer remains open.

As the result of a chance introduction at a political dinner in Suffolk in 1991, Robert Grimsey, a horticulturist then working with

Plants are grown on in the nursery.

Seed frames are the starting point.

Notcutts Nurseries (sadly no longer trading) at Woodbridge in Suffolk, wrote to ask if the garden was open to the public. He explained that he was about to build a National Collection of Horse Chestnuts and Buckeyes on a two-and-a-half-acre field adjoining his home. With our enthusiastic encouragement, he has since developed an almost proprietorial interest in our collection, to the extent that he is authorised to buy on sight any plants that are unrepresented at Thenford. He has also contributed many of the more than eighty *Aesculus* that we have, including the *Aesculus hippocastanum* 'Monstrosa' I mentioned in Chapter Twelve and *Aesculus turbinata* 'Marble Chip', a striking variegated form of Japanese horse chestnut raised in the US. When that arrived with us, there were just four young grafted plants of it in the UK. Robert also collected seeds at Thenford when he ran the International Dendrology Society's seed exchange scheme a few years ago.

At the 1996 Conservative Party Conference, Anne sat next to John Taylor, the vice president of the National Union of Conservative and Unionist Associations. His family business deals in bulbs. After the conference, Anne and I were surprised but delighted to receive large quantities of six different daffodils – *Narcissus* 'W. p. Milner', 'Suzy', 'Quail', 'Chanterelle', 'Jetfire' and 'Pipit'. We had decided, after clearing the yew avenue, not to plant anything that intruded into the mown green space. The gift of daffodils changed our minds and they bring a sparkling spring perspective.

Early in our arboretum's development, we became friendly with Michael Heathcoat Amory who, like us, was building a collection of oaks. Before his sad death in 2016, he had created what must be one of the world's largest collections of oaks at Chevithorne Barton in Devon. He was advised and encouraged by Allen Coombes of the Sir Harold Hillier Gardens who was responsible for the entire collection there but had a particular specialisation in oaks. Michael was combing the world for additions and gathered a small circle of friends, including me, to help fund Allen's acorn expeditions to eastern Asia and Mexico, often in collaboration with the International Oak Society. Not all of Allen's introductions, particularly from southern Mexico, proved hardy enough to survive but many did and it has been particularly satisfying to pass on our surplus seedlings to other distinguished gardens and arboreta including Antony, Blenheim, Dumbleton Hall, Hergest Croft and Stonor Park. I re-read recently the list of oaks I gave to Anthony Cheetham, a fellow publisher, to add to his collection in Gloucestershire: *Quercus macrocarpa, laceyi, rysophylla, rugosa, laurina, mexicana, gravesii, polymorpha, crassipes* and *infectoria* subsp. *veneris*. These are just a few examples that we have spread widely among our friends. Inevitably there will be disappointments. Their recent introduction means we don't yet have enough knowledge for an informed view of their performance and survivability in the long term. For some years Thenford kept pace with Chevithorne Barton's collection of oaks but latterly we conceded leadership. Michael had 465 different oaks. With only 370, we are some way behind – but he didn't have our 342 different snowdrops.

The latest package of acorns arrived as we were finalising the text of this book. Jamie Compton has taken over from Michael the responsibility for organising the meticulous distribution of acorns collected. This package had come from Béatrice Chassé, co-founder of Arboretum des Pouyouleix, a sixty-acre arboretum with more than 300 species of oaks at Saint-Jory-de-Chalais in the Dordogne from whom we have received many acorns over the years. There is real excitement in establishing the list of newcomers, in preparing the labels, filling the root trainers and planting the acorns as fast as possible because many are already showing their tap root. To explain the excitement that is such a satisfying part of garden mania, let me record the sixteen different species of oak that I planted on a Sunday morning: *Quercus aliena, championii, chapmanii, gilva, glauca, hypophaea, liaoi, longinux, morii, myrsinifolia, pachyloma, sessilifolia, stenophylloides, variabilis, spinosa* and *spinosa* subsp. *miyabei*. By the end of May 2016 six had germinated.

In the 1990s, we visited John Vanderplank of Tynings nursery in

Aesculus hippocastanum 'Monstrosa'.

Quercus durata.

Quercus rivasmartinezii.

Quercus semecarpifolia.

Quercus dentata 'Carl Ferris Miller'.

Quercus rubra 'Aurea'.

Quercus rotundifolia.

Quercus argyrotricha.

Quercus affinis.

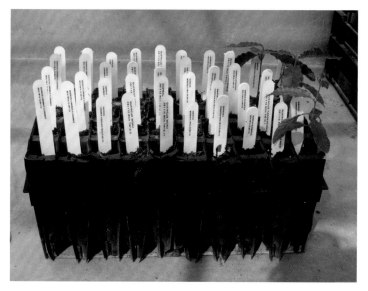

1. Acorns sown into root trainers.

3. Transferred into individual pots.

2. Almost ready for potting.

4. The next phase of life begins.

Somerset to see the National Collection of passion flowers (*Passiflora*) there. The journey was worth it for that experience alone, particularly now they are creating a massive collection of climbers. But as we were chatting we caught sight of rows and rows of box plants. It turned out that they were a collection formed by local enthusiast Ron Kew who had nowhere to house them. The outcome was inevitable: forty-three new additions joined our collection. The story did not end there. While writing this book, I contacted John who told me that some of the collection never came because Ron had, at that time, hoped to build it up again. We agreed that they would join their original colleagues. At the last count we now have fifty-five different types of box. The last three, *Buxus henryi*, *B. rugulosa* var. *intermedia* and *B. sinica* var. *insularis* were selected by Tony Kirkham, head of the arboretum at the Royal Botanic Gardens, Kew, for Marcus Agius, chairman of Kew's trustees, to give to us on a visit.

Jeanette Fryer wrote, with Bertil Hylmö, *Cotoneasters: A Comprehensive Guide to Shrubs for Flowers, Fruit and Foliage*. She is an acknowledged authority who had created an extraordinary collection of cotoneasters. Over the years we had bought plants from her, and enjoyed her visit to check our labelling on the ground. In 2011 she wrote to say she had decided to give up her nursery and intended to transfer the collection to Exbury Gardens. But she wanted us to have the chance to augment our own collection. So we were able to add, in groups of three, eighty different cotoneasters. We now have 350, with many others added from seeds collected by Keith Rushforth, Chris Chadwell or sent by Géza Kósa from the Institute of Ecology and Botany at Vácrátót, near the Danube an hour north of Budapest.

We have been building the collection of snowdrops that Anne talked about in Chapter Two for many years. We met Carolyn and Henry Elwes through mutual friends and they helped start us on our galanthophile journey with offerings from their collection at Colesbourne in Gloucestershire. The name Elwes is, of course, one of the most famous in the *Galanthus* world. Henry's great-grandfather, Henry John Elwes, discovered Elwes's snowdrop (*Galanthus elwesii*) in Turkey in 1874. Henry and Carolyn's gifts, and a careful survey of specialist growers, helped us lay the foundations of a significant collection. Then, out of the blue in 2013, we received a letter from Margaret MacLennan. Together with her husband David, a retired British Ambassador who had served in Lebanon and Qatar, she had amassed a collection of more than 1000 different varieties of snowdrops to form the National Collection. Her letter simply asked if we would be willing to house spares from her extensive programme of chipping and scaling bulbs. She offered to support our staff if we agreed. Some letters answer themselves. Now, we have some 342 different snowdrops.

Hostas are very happy in our soil and the variety of their size, shape and colour make them invaluable for filling the gaps in the borders and shrubbery. Indeed, at the extreme end we have *Hosta* 'Pandora's Box' in the Trough Garden. It is so small it borders on invisible. Over time, hostas are breeders. New introductions appear year by year. We have developed a relationship with Bowden Hostas of

Three *buxus* from Marcus Agius.

Galanthus elwesii.

Small *Hosta* 'Pandora's Box'.

Okehampton, Devon, who have had a conspicuous presence at horticultural shows, including centre stage at Chelsea Flower Show in 2015. We buy their magnificent pots of show plants at the end of the season. Financially, it becomes attractive if we are able to divide each of the thirty or so potfuls into seven or eight rooted subdivisions. Bowden also took over the specialist fern nursery Richards Ferns in 2016. Over the years we had bought ferns for our damper, shadier areas and their closing down sale brought fifty additions to our collection.

There can be a sad note to these substantial acquisitions. In 2015, Evolution Plants, Tom Mitchell's exciting and innovative nursery at Bradford on Avon in Wiltshire, closed its doors when Tom decided his skills weren't suited to running a nursery. The word spread that the stock was heading for the bonfire on a given date but was available for collection by anyone with the energy to do so. We picked up more than 150 different plants including five wild-collected species of *Rudbeckia* and another five species of *Dierama*. At least Tom's vision will live on in the gardens of several owners who remain grateful.

Rhaphiolepis umbellata.

Not all the offerings we receive are about collections. My childhood was enriched by time spent on the beaches of the Gower Peninsular in South Wales and, in particular, Langland. In September 2007, seventy-six-year-old Norma Wedlake wrote from Langland explaining that she had no space for seven Corsican pines (*Pinus nigra* subsp. *laricio*). She had not been well, had nowhere to plant them and was looking for a home for them. Her request, was, of course, granted with pleasure. We received with equal pleasure rooted cuttings of box taken from the original Heseltine family home in Swansea that were collected by Elizabeth Marks, my aunt. Another singleton, *Cercis canadensis* 'Lavender Twist', came from John Jackson, Headmaster of Warwick School, as a thank you for a speech I made because two sons of neighbouring farmers, Philip and Elizabeth Bywater, were pupils there in 2008. An unusual small shrub from Japan, a Yeddo hawthorn (*Rhaphiolepis umbellata*), was sent by Henry and Tessa Keswick from their fine collection at Oare in Wiltshire.

Certainly, the largest boost to our collection, as well as one of the most recent, came as the result of an email from Robert Mattock in 2015. As the MP for Henley, I was very familiar with Mattocks Nursery at Nuneham Courtenay outside Oxford. The family specialised in roses and we had called on Robert to advise us (see Chapter Eleven). He had helped Anne select the range of white roses for the Rose Garden and made a significant contribution when we replanted it after George Carter's new design. Robert had learnt his trade in the family business but played a diminishing part in its direction after he chose his own professional pathway. However, his love of roses endured and he wanted to preserve the family's extensive collection. It is this collection – and Robert's additions to it – that have now been incorporated into our rose collection.

The message in his email was simple: he needed a permanent home for the Mattock collection and he invited us and Tim Whiteley, who had created his woodland garden at nearby Evenley, to provide them. The arrangement was straightforward. Robert would give us the plants, help with their location and have access to them for his use in the future. He would also provide a large number of rooted stock onto which we would graft new additions that he anticipated would be supplied by fellow international enthusiasts. Both of us agreed, and at the time of going to press virtually all of our new roses have been planted in their new homes. Before the Mattock roses arrived, we already had a considerable collection because our large number of mature yew and holly trees make wonderful hosts to the vigorous climber and rambler species. Without duplicates, the present collection of roses is in the region of 400, including 100 different species. Robert now combines his extensive academic and speaking career with his continuing interest in the development of our joint collection into one of the most comprehensive in the UK.

Something we never envisaged is Thenford being used as a field station for scientific research. Over the years, we have raised plants from rose seeds collected in the wild by several plant collectors working in China and Central Asia. As part of his research into the *Silk*

Rosa 'Ispahan'.

Rosa moyesii.

Rosa woodsii var. *fendleri*.

Rosa 'Hunter' (*R. rugosa* cultivar).

Rosa × *odorata* 'Mutabilis'

Rosa 'Minnehaha' (Rambler 1905).

Rosa 'Félicité et Perpétue' (Rambler 1827).

Rosa × *harisonii* 'Williams Double Yellow'.

Our rehoused cacti collection now in their dozens.

Road Hybrids, Robert is seeking to fill a significant gap in the knowledge of the phylogenetics – the family tree – of the Central Asian rose species, the damask rose (*Rosa × damascena*). The project is tracking the transmigration in this rose of remontancy – the important horticultural ability to flower recurrently – from its origins in Persia to the west where it appeared in Roman gardens in classical times. It is already established that one of the parents of *Rosa × damascena*, the parent carrying the remontant gene, is most likely to be one of the *Musk* roses. However, until the advent of DNA analysis ten or so years ago, classification of the group was thought too complex to merit useful investigation.

Our methodology is to subject material from either the wild-collected plants already established in our collection, or material derived from wild-sourced seed currently being collected in Central Asia, to ISSR-PCR-DNA analysis. Wild-collected material is essential to avoid the risk of infection by hybridisation which occurs in plants in cultivation. One 100-gram sample from the seed germinated here has been sent to the University of Bath for testing and analysis.

The Mattock research programme hopes to establish whether these plants, which appear different to the eye, are in fact disparate species or are genetically identical. All importantly, it will also show which species or their naturally occurring hybrids may be used to in-

troduce or increase recurrent flowering, or remontancy, in this economically important plant. Not only will this work horticulturally define, for the first time, the poorly classified but very important range of damask garden roses, but better understanding will enable nurserymen in the rose oil and rose water business in the Middle East, Central Asia, India and China to increase production perhaps threefold. Rose water is used in huge volumes in religious ceremony, medicines and cuisine throughout the Islamic world.

We had just concluded the arrangements to recover the Mattock collection when we received a message enquiring if we would be interested in a collection of cacti. Sadly, we had to decline. At least that was what I thought we had agreed. Sometime later, I was wandering through one of our greenhouses and there they were. It transpired that Darren had met Peter and Jeanie Elliott of Warkworth, near Banbury, who had made the offer, and he couldn't resist. Darren had brought with him a small personal collection of cacti when he left Kew. This was too good a chance to double the number. They are wonderful but our first challenge is to find out what they actually are, occupying, as they do, a dedicated section of a greenhouse.

From our earliest days at Thenford we have used black engraved labels for our trees and shrubs. At the time we got started, Charlie Shelburne was labelling his own collection using a Gravograph system. In May 1978 we agreed that he would provide us with engraved laminated black four-inch by two-inch labels for our initial Hillier order at a cost of 32p each. Shortly afterwards, we decided to buy our own machine and opted for the basic manual model. The process is simple. You select letters or numbers from a tray to make the name, slot them into a platform, then press one end of a guide into the engraved slot on each letter. By following the trace, an electric drill connected to the guide then engraves an identical pattern on the plastic plate. In 2015 we moved on to a computer-controlled model which we first saw in Stephen Hester's garden at Broughton Grange. We should have taken his advice to trade up earlier but the many long hours of grinding had a therapeutic quality as an escape from the incessant flow of paperwork from politics. It also amused our grandchildren who went away with their own personalised labels.

Since the collection widened to include bulbs and herbaceous plants, both in the greenhouses, the nursery and outside in the garden, we have tried many different labels. We have used aluminium labels with pencil markings that last well. Our experience of 'everlasting' pens is that they prove to be anything but. We use the traditional plastic labels – usually white but coloured if that helps distinguish different groupings. For identification, we use a handheld Brother machine to create stick-on marking. We have found, however, that the plastic labels deteriorate with exposure to ultraviolet light which means that they snap at the slightest touch. That has proved particularly disappointing because we persuaded a manufacturer to incorporate a green dye into their eight-inch white labels, so they would be less conspicuous amongst the herbaceous plants. They didn't survive long. We have discovered that a twelve-inch piece of bamboo with a wide code number wrapped round the top is useful for bulbs during their flowering period. The important lesson is to label everything with permanent identification the moment it arrives. Human memory is frail. Many things are similar or can only be identified when in flower or fruit. Many labels are insecure and detachable and, to our cost, we've learnt that it's a mistake not to establish permanent records.

Computer system replaced the old Gravograph.

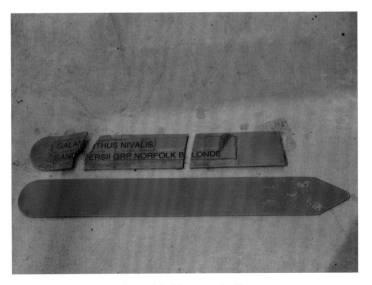

Green label intact and split.

Michael making labels.

This is doubly true before things are planted out in their final homes, where there are new enemies. We have a rule – as with many rules, there are mistakes – that nothing is planted without a permanent identification. But that isn't enough. We lost labels because we used plastic-coated wire that was too thin. To our amateur eyes it seemed strong enough, but we had ignored the wear and tear of years of wind and weather. Our own pruning can be a hazard if labels are attached to the end of branches that are pruned away in late summer. We aim to fix labels firmly to the trunk of a tree at about eye height, or close to the centre of a shrub where it can be seen when the plant is in leaf.

Throughout 2015 we worked with Hugh Angus following his retirement as Head of Tree Collections at Westonbirt in Gloucestershire to authenticate our collection and prepare it for digitalisation. Every tree and shrub has had to be inspected and, hopefully, identified. Missing labels are replaced and updated.

There are two ways to assess our endeavours to keep track of our collection. We can be pleased with the identification of so high a proportion; or we can despair at the small number that remain unlabelled and unknown. There are also many questions. Were the labels accurate in the first place? Nurseries have been known to make mistakes. Labels fall or are cut off, and are then later attached to the nearest thing that looks right – or just the nearest thing! A magnificent flourishing plant can turn out to be understock, with a spindly dead graft long-since departed this world, carrying a time-worn label. Many plants have synonyms (alternative names). You can discover that three different names are in fact referring to the same plant in the collection. Finding an expert with the knowledge to identify the minute differences that separate forms of species is the most frustrating, if understandable, difficulty. Fortunately, we've had help from Roy Lancaster, Keith Rushforth and Allen Coombes – but there aren't many like

Twelve-inch bamboo marker for snowdrops.

Label correctly placed at chest height.

Our original loose leaf record.

The computer age takes over.

them. Listening to the often quite heated arguments of specialists as they visit the collection demonstrates the scale of the problem. Hugh's dedication and expertise has proved invaluable.

Regarding the plant names in this book, we have agonised over which source to rely on for correct botanical names. Different names may be applied to the same plant (synonym). On the other hand, homonyms are the same name applied to different types. Re-classification of names can also change the familiar to the unknown. In the end, we have decided to follow, as best we can, up-to-date nomenclature used by the Royal Horticultural Society. The website www.thenfordarboretum will list our plants and be regularly updated.

The creation of our arboretum coincides with history's fastest and most pervasive revolution in human communication. Only thirty-five years ago we recorded the location of our plants in card boxes and loose-leaf files. It was quite exhilarating to watch the system expand as, year after year, another file, with its date carefully sellotaped onto the cover, was added to our records. In the mid 1980s we set out with pen and paper to check that there actually were plants where the records claimed. The communication revolution could quite easily have passed us by as others converted our manuscript notes into finished and polished prose. I had regarded computers with deep suspicion, coupled almost certainly with the fear that I was incapable of mastering these techniques. It was a visit one day to a primary school that proved the turning point. I saw row upon row of four-year-olds tapping away, totally in charge, conjuring up letters, numbers, and images at the tap of their tiny fingers. With some apprehension, it dawned on me that I was not that stupid and that, if they could do it, so could I. So the garden drew me into the computer age. The ability to find a location, date of planting, supplying nurseries and any appropriate notes at the tap of a 'Find' button opened up a new world. Of course, as all those children already knew, this was the future. But the explosion of technical options was at an early stage.

I do not remember precisely when the word satellite crossed my horizon. Given my days as Minister for Aerospace and Shipping in the 1970s, I had had an interest in space. I helped to create the European Space Agency but I had never seen a link between the arboretum and the whiz-kiddery of all those signals and satellites flying around out there. Mixing metaphors, the penny finally dropped in February 1999. We commissioned Ordnance Survey to update the part of their map that covered the arboretum and to survey-in 150 of our early plantings. As this book describes, we were engaged in several large projects at the time and the work was put on hold until we returned to it in February 2011.

There was one mistake we did not make. We were determined not to invent our own system so we sought a company that had already moved up the learning curve through experience on other people's projects. We chose VantagePoint Cartographics who had developed an appropriate system for the Birmingham Botanical Gardens, the National Memorial Arboretum and Charles Howick's remarkable collection at Howick Hall Gardens near Alnwick, Northumberland.

The system we chose incorporated and linked a database, a visual map and photographic records, including full details of the tiniest bulb and the largest tree. The earlier paper records are now redundant. Pointing a handheld device at any plant will reveal its entry in the database, including photographs. The basis of the system is a GPS survey of each plant. The next stage is to identify each plant physically and link it to our existing catalogue. Darren checks the botanical nomenclature and passes the details to VantagePoint to update the digital map. Once completed, the process delivers a searchable map, which can be viewed on a handheld device or computer.

So far, we have named and awarded an accession number to 5000 plants. There are still several thousand to be checked. Given that most trees are singletons and that shrubs are planted in groups of three or five, our view is that the collection now numbers more than 3000 different varieties of trees and shrubs. Most of the herbaceous plants and bulbs are yet to be included.

Chapter Fourteen

ACQUISITIONS

An arrangement was made… a scarlet oak and a southern beech then arrived from the Duchy of Cornwall nursery. No planting was ever conducted with such care.

by Michael Heseltine

THENFORD
The Creation of an
English Garden

I HAVE LEFT TO LAST THE MOST PERSONAL part of collecting. Distinguished visitors, specialist groups and friends deserve recognition, above all for their gifts. There is no better present, no more permanent memorial for an anniversary or birthday, than to receive a plant. We try to replace casualties and to reward our friends' generosity with appropriate labels. We have noticed that labels with people's names on them provoke others to ask how can they get one too. We owe so much pleasure to the generosity of others.

No large garden or arboretum is complete without its memorial trees celebrating a visit of the great and good. Ours is no exception – even if we may have been somewhat economical with the truth in our recording of the events.

Anne was staying with friends in the Beaufort country, expecting to hunt the following morning. Dense fog put paid to that and, having discarded her hunting coat for an old jacket, she found an advertisement for a local demolition yard in the pocket. It was another of those opportunities not to be missed. Once there, when she asked about the availability of granite setts, she was driven to an old railway station and told: 'If you want them you have to take the lot.' The deal was done.

In the eastern courtyard of our house, Quinlan Terry had created an office and a garage, outside of which there was a muddy patch. The granite setts were ideal for a proper hard standing; we enclosed

Fiona Heyward's contribution to a 'Tree Fund' on a signficant birthday.

them with stone pillars which the local builders copied from Quinlan's Summer House. There were, however, many setts left over.

Prince Charles, who was riding with the Bicester on our land shortly afterwards, spotted them. The Master, Ian Farquhar, phoned to ask about their availability. An arrangement was made and the surplus setts went to Highgrove. A scarlet oak (*Quercus coccinea*) and a Dombey's southern beech (*Nothofagus dombeyi*) then arrived from the Duchy of Cornwall nursery. No planting was ever conducted with such care. Our most distinguished labels were engraved.

Prime Ministers have to appear to be enthusiasts when the ceremonial spade is thrust into their hands. We can score five and a President, if you are prepared to permit a degree of political licence. None of them in truth actually planted anything. Our friendship with the Douglas-Homes and their visits are treasured memories. I had entered active politics in a wave of enthusiasm for a new and radical approach for the Conservative Party, heralded by the election of Ted Heath as leader. We did not get to know the Douglas-Homes until long after Alec's premiership ended in 1964. He was a great countryman and gardener, and he and his wife Elizabeth brought seedlings with them – a mountain clematis (*Clematis montana*) – when they first came to stay. This clematis is a rampant climber, available now in a wide range of colours from pure white to dark red. We first saw it on the front drive of The Hirsel, the Douglas-Home's Scottish home. Anne particularly remembers one weekend when they were with us. We collapsed into armchairs, exhausted after a long walk. After his tea, Alec said 'Come on, Michael, there's a bit we haven't seen.' Off we went, only returning when it was dark. We were delighted to receive an ornamental bramble – *Rubus* 'Benenden' – as thanks for the visit.

Ted Heath certainly visited in 1992 and was appropriately – some would say unaccustomedly – polite. He never actually knew that we planted a *Pinus* × *densithunbergii* to celebrate the event but it seems a not unreasonable licence. Margaret Thatcher never came and almost certainly was quite unaware that her one-time environment spokesman was actually trying to create a bit of it. The facts of how she came to contribute to our collection are simple. She was invited to address both Houses of Congress and to hold talks with President Regan in 1985. The flight to the US in a Vickers VC10 included Geoffrey Howe, Foreign Secretary, myself as Defence Secretary, and Anne. It was probably singularly inappropriate – during a discussion of UK strategic policy – to request access to Chequers to take a cutting from one of the famous box plants. I was able to satisfy myself that I had a 'yes' and no one tried to stop my later excursion to nick the necessary cuttings. They flourish in our collection thirty years later.

It was during that visit to the US that I met Senator John Warner. Distinguished in his own right, he had added Elizabeth Taylor to his achievements by marrying her in 1976. I knew that his state of Virginia was home to the red buckeye (*Aesculus pavia*). 'Senator,' I said, 'is there the slightest chance that I could obtain some conkers?' Through typical American generosity a significant number duly arrived. We have a fine specimen today. Some years later I met John again and

Granite setts in the courtyard.

Nothofagus dombeyi.

Quercus coccinea.

Nothofagus dombeyi.

Aesculus pavia.

Pinus × densithunbergii.

Fraxinus profunda.

The Chequers box (*Buxus sempervirens*).

Gewürztraminer Grand Cru Froehn, 1988
(Jean Becker)
Savigny-lès-Beaune Dominode, 1987
(Bruno Clair)

Gravlax and Citrus Salad
Yoghurt Dressing

Suprême of Corn Fed Chicken
with a Tarragon Crust
Redcurrant Sauce
New Potatoes with Chives
Garden Vegetables
Mixed Leaf Salad

Summer Pudding
Crème Fraîche Ice Cream

Cheese

Coffee

10 Downing Street
23rd July 1995

President Bush's menu card...

...with this message on the back.

during the course of our conversation he asked 'Did Mrs Thatcher like the chestnuts?' I hadn't the heart to tell him!

Interestingly enough, John Major also had a double whammy. He came with Norma in 1993 to visit us when I was confined to barracks after a heart attack. We cannot pretend that the prime ministerial foot ever touched a spade but over twenty years later the *Fraxinus profunda* celebrates the visit. President Bush visited the United Kingdom in 1995 and was the principal guest at a dinner in his honour at 10 Downing Street. I had a word with John. To my delight, the next day he handed me the menu card with a message from the President. No prizes for guessing that a *Quercus × bushii* was added to the arboretum.

A very personal gift came from Charlie Price, the American Ambassador at the time of the Westland Affair in 1985–6. This is not the place to fan old embers but because an American company's wish to purchase a British defence contractor was the background to the saga, it was all too easy for my critics to portray my position – quite wrongly – as anti-American. After the event Charlie came to see the arboretum and asked if he could give me a tree. After wrestling for some time with the pronunciation of *Pinus* we settled for three paperbark maples. 'If I had been you,' he said, 'I would have done exactly what you did'. He was a great ambassador.

No story of the transatlantic import into our arboretum can leave out our contact with Barry Goldwater, the US Senator who represented Arizona for five terms and was the Republican nominee in the 1964 presidential election. He had tried to send me a *Pinus arizonica*. In March 1985 I had to write to tell him it had been confiscated by HM Revenue & Customs. He expressed his regrets and promised a replacement hidden in his luggage on his next visit. To protect his rep-

Visit of Charlie Price.

Acer griseum.

Barry Goldwater's letter...

utation against enquiry by the appropriate enforcement authorities, I hasten to add that nothing ever happened.

The flora and fauna of China is legendary. Britain's great gardens have been enriched over more than two centuries by the finds of intrepid plant collectors. We ourselves have benefited greatly from the generosity of the Shanghai Botanical Garden which we first visited in 1973 and from which we have received many different seeds. Without pretending any official or personal endorsement, we have taken the liberty of planting trees to celebrate the visit of two very distinguished Chinese officials to Thenford. In 1992, before he became Premier, Zhu Rongji led a delegation to the UK with Madame Wu Yi. I discovered that Foreign Office hospitality had committed them to a Sunday tour of the Cotswolds – and so I hijacked the visit. An ash (*Fraxinus sieboldiana*) commemorates the occasion. In November 1996, as I mentioned in Chapter Five, we were able to entertain Vice Premier Li Lanqing here. The walnut (*Juglans mandshurica*) commemorates the day in the part of the arboretum that's planted only with trees and shrubs from China and which Roy Lancaster helped to design in 1986. We have no shame about the licence we have taken in accrediting trees to these visits. Most politicians would feel deeply satisfied if these were the worst of their exaggerations!

David Cameron came frequently when he was an undergraduate and friend of our daughter Alexandra. These visits have yet to be commemorated arboreally.

Many friends have given, volunteered to purchase or turned up with goodies they have grown, tools they find useful, and even garden seats. Alexandra and Nick gave one and we have another given by Annabel's four children. Friends not only bring gifts: they bring

March 13ᵗʰ 1985

Dear Senator Goldwater,

I bring you news of a sad ending to a most generous gesture on your part.

American pines are virtually impossible to import into this country. Apparently there are certain diseases which we don't have associated with pines and which we are fearful would spread rapidly in so constrained a country. The importation authorities and I slogged it out for three days but although I was able to achieve a stay of execution whilst the battle of words raged in the end it was I fear total victory for the machine. The trees died at dawn.

It so happens I have British born versions of your pine – Pinus Eldarica and I intend to plant them alongside a small commemorative plaque recording your generosity and their short but troubled life.

With every good wish
Yours sincerely

...and Michael's note.

Fraxinus sieboldiana commemorates the 1992 visit of Zhu Rongji and Madame Wu Yi.

Juglans mandshurica for the 1996 visit of Li Lanqing.

advice, they bring ideas. There are two familiar approaches to this. 'Bloody cheek.' Or 'Did you hear what he/she said?' We take the opposite view. Everything is worth listening to. Rather arrogantly, we have sufficient confidence in what we've done to welcome criticism. We think about suggestions and are happy to adopt those we like. It is hardly surprising that most garden design is a version of someone else's ideas. People have been creating gardens in Europe for well over 1000 years. One hopes to leave some personal stamp – but all those coffee table books, all those visits to mature gardens… of course they influence and inspire. Let's be frank. Sometimes we copy. There are many permutations on these themes: the *allée* at Hidcote, the rill in Canada, the benches at Boughton, the auricular theatre at Waddesdon. Could the designers of those wonderful things deny a parentage for their own projects? During our search for ideas, it was a particular pleasure when I was Secretary of State for the Environment to invite the head gardeners from the Royal Parks to show them that their political master at least knew the difference between a spade and a fork.

Come September we begin the planting season, which we aim to finish by March. That's usually optimistic. By then the grass and weeds force us to divert to maintenance. The planting process is relatively simple and consists of compiling lists of suitable plants in the standing beds. If our purpose was to create spectacular borders, vistas or landscapes, the process would be very different. Designs would be conceived, plants ordered and the work put in hand. But we are collectors and the objective is to accumulate the widest possible range, from

Dear Mummy and Daddy

SEASON'S GREETINGS

lots of love

Nick Alexandra and Molly

X

Sold in aid of
THE BRITISH RED CROSS

A Registered Charity.

The British Red Cross gives skilled and impartial care to people
in need and crisis – in their homes and in the community, at
home and abroad, in peace and in war.

Alexandra, Nick and Molly gave a seat.

Visit of gardeners from the Royal Parks.

the smallest bulbs to the tallest trees. Some of our sources – such as the nursery trade – are obvious and conventional. But over the previous year we will have received many gifts from visitors and friends, we will have propagated new additions and bulked up our existing stock, we will have helped to finance seed collecting expeditions, we will have ordered seeds from specialist societies or other arboreta across the world, and we will have grown herbaceous plants from our own seed or divided clumps into larger groupings.

If you're looking for them, there are many sources of seed. There are websites, commercial catalogues and specialists. Sadly, Chris Chadwell, from whom we obtained many seeds, announced on his website that he has had to close because his suppliers in the Himalayas 'are getting too old and new rules and regulations mean that it will be increasingly difficult to find sources – it's very much the end of an era.' There are many of us in his debt.

Many specialist nurseries are owned by collectors who will offer plants under their own collection number. Farmers-turned-horticulturalists Sue and Bleddyn Wynn-Jones at Crûg Farm Nursery, which nestles above the Menai Strait in North Wales, have amassed a mouth-watering collection. They collected many themselves, particularly in Taiwan, and their plants enjoy the favourable climate at Crûg, with its limited frost exposure. A visit is worth the journey. Few places offer more than forty species of *Hydrangea* in their catalogue.

Many arboreta or specialist societies offer lists of seeds, collected either in the wild or from their own plants. Our collection has been

Géza Kósa and Erzsébet Fráter on our buggy.

particularly enriched by plants grown from seeds received from St Andrews Botanic Garden, the Shanghai Botanical Garden, the Taiwan Forestry Research Institute and the Hungarian Academy of Sciences Botanic Garden. Over the years Kew, Edinburgh, Bedgebury, Westonbirt and Wisley have been generous with advice and plants.

The RHS Plant Finder is, of course, the invaluable tool for anyone seeking a particular plant. Naturally, there is an element of luck in the nature of the product. Nurserymen list what they have available *at the time.* Things sell out, crops fail, disease strikes but usually the system delivers and certainly, as we've learned, it's the place to start.

There is no way to know in advance what success rate to expect from seed propagation. On several occasions we have bought other people's collections when, for whatever reason, the owner has decided to give up. Armed with relevant lists – including number availability, ultimate size, any information about tenderness, planting conditions and autumn colour – we mark out new positions with bamboo canes to indicate their appropriate homes. We want the finished planting to look as good as possible but, let's face it, many varieties are rare in cultivation because they are pretty drab; interest in them stems from their rarity. But this rather haphazard approach has produced some visually exciting plantings and, of course, we do adopt a much more conventional design concept when planning our borders.

Finding homes for new plants has relatively few guidelines. We plant single trees and only one of any name. This rule has become stricter as space becomes tighter. We plant the larger shrubs in threes and the smaller ones in fives. We fill the available space with herbaceous plants. We have learnt the value of the early advice we were given: that impact needs scale. But if this advice encourages the use of herbaceous plants or small shrubs to create this effect, it leaves the obvious dilemma over where to plant trees. We try to site a single specimen where it will mature. This means finding an open space which the tree can gradually fill. Certainly any proximity to a neighbouring canopy will encourage a young tree to grow to the light. Single trees will be exposed to the wind unless neighbours can be planted and later cleared or a practical shelterbelt grown nearby.

We are fortunate with our soil. Not only will virtually anything grow, except the most acid-loving plants, but we have generous rainfall, significant springs and streamside planting areas. Of course, we didn't listen to those who told us we would never grow rhododendrons. Encouraged by the existence of groups of *Rhododendron ponticum* and with generous peat enhancement of our soil, we were determined to try. The rhododendrons have long since moved to Exmoor where Anne owned a small farm, and thrive happily there in the peaty soil. More recently, the rhododendron that John and Penny Gummer gave us is growing well. Camellias flourish in some of our more sheltered, damper locations.

This book is not a 'how to' instruction manual, although every gardener should have one. Planting is not a question of just dumping things in holes. Take trouble and you will be rewarded. There are lessons we have learnt. The hole should be significantly

Previous page Betula utilis var. *jacquemontii* 'Grayswood ghost'. *Above Liriodendron tulipifera* 'Aureomarginatum'.

Quercus rubra.

Cedrus atlantica (Glauca Group) 'Glauca'.

bigger than the pot in which the plant is growing. We create a square hole to encourage roots to spread. Compost and fertiliser are added where appropriate. If necessary, use a stake to ensure that the rooted plant is stable and cannot be disturbed by wind. Above all, remember the enemies. You are planting a potential source of food (particularly in winter) for rabbits, hares and – increasingly – deer. They have few natural predators and can wreck young saplings overnight. So know your enemy and protect against them.

Grey squirrels are devastating for us. They can strip the bark from a prized specimen well above any protection and, if they strip the tree's entire circumference, this girdling or ring-barking will kill it. We are particularly aggravated by the behaviour of young squirrels in the spring. They will nip the young shoots of chestnuts, leaving about twelve inches of growth hanging straight down. These foreign intruders may have a Walt Disney appeal in London parks but to us they are Public Enemy Number One – to borrow the old FBI term – and are shot without hesitation. To indicate the scale of the problem, we have shot or trapped nearly 300 in just six months. They have largely destroyed England's indigenous red squirrels but we are not going to let them destroy our trees without a fight. We are keen ornithologists and were particularly enraged to find that every nesting box had had its entrance enlarged by squirrels and the nest destroyed. As a result of our efforts, the small birds we treasure will be safer in the future.

Nesting box entrance ravaged by squirrels.

Understandably, all of us focus on the early stages of new planting although appropriate attention should also be applied to watering, feeding, weeding and formative pruning. How often do you hear people say that we are only planting for the next generation? Nothing could be further from the truth. Anne and I began nearly forty years ago, when we were about forty. Photographs show us alongside trees we planted then, with their dates. Anyone planting in early middle age can still expect a great deal of satisfaction. One of our memories may help. Many years ago we visited an experiment at Long Ashton Research Station. There were three rows of identical trees. The first row was growing with uncontrolled vegetation around it. The second row had had circles of vegetation sprayed out to about twelve inches. The ground around the third row had been clear-sprayed. The trees in row three were double the height of row one. It showed us that with care and attention, you can make great strides with your planting and enjoy the rewards in a shorter time than you might imagine.

So we could end this book 'Job done', as the saying goes. But of course gardening is not like that. As we said in the Introduction, we have presented a snapshot of our garden which, by its very nature, conveys a fixed image. Gardens abide by no such rules. Just the tasks of maintenance will mean changes as young trees crowd each other out in the battle for light and space. Plants will die or lose their appeal. There are duplicates, sometimes triplicates, which will have to give way as the demands of a growing collection need space.

There are the areas we haven't told you about. Lanning Roper's continuing advice rings down the years. We have been in a hurry and pursued projects that we were then unable to maintain. The Bog Garden at the extreme southeast of the arboretum is not all we hoped it would be. Maintenance, or the lack of it, has had the better of us. We will have to launch a counter attack against the ruthless forces of nature but we are unapologetic because the trees planted – *Betula, Metasequoia, Taxodium* – have since matured. We have giant *Gunnera* and clumps of *Hydrangea* with which to work. We need to achieve an easier access to stream banks and there is Veitch's bamboo (*Sasa veitchii*) to eliminate near Alan's Fall. This is small change in the shape of things, and the maturity of the surrounding area now needs only the determination to get on with it.

There are projects yet to finish and others yet to start. Yet again we have brought things back from the flea market: a pair of magnificent purple marble pillars to build into a revised endpoint for the herbaceous borders. We have a pair of cows from the 2002 CowParade in London – auctioned for charity after being displayed on the capital's streets – to place in the arboretum, along with the sculpture used by the Millennium Commission to celebrate Sustrans, its national cycle way. After forty years, we are now short of space but there is still one substantial area where we could create a significant feature. We will wait to be inspired.

A hundred years from now our trees will still be here. We hope others will enjoy them then as much as we do now.

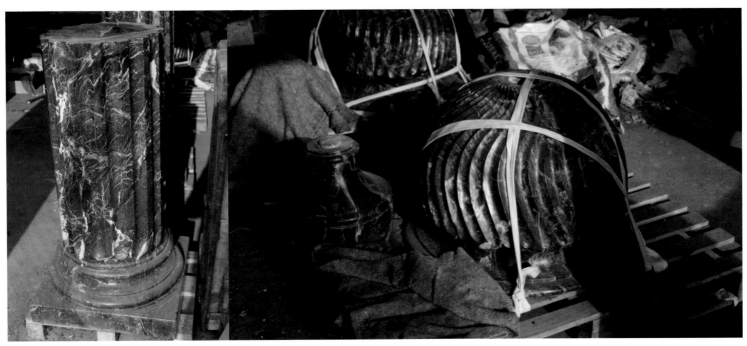

Marble pillars from the flea market.

Charity cows from the CowParade.

SCULPTURE GARDEN

JAY BATTLE ARBS (*contemporary British*)
'The Husk' – limestone on steel base
Provenance: Henley Festival, 1997

COPIES FROM THE TEMPLES
OF ANGKOR WAT, SIEM REAP,
CAMBODIA
Medium head of Yaksha – sandstone
Great Head of Deva – sandstone
Provenance: Artisans d'Angkor

DZINTRA JANSONE (*Latvian 1945-*)
Bust of Lenin – bronze, *c.*1979
*Provenance: removed from a town square in
Preili, Latvia, after the fall of Communism*

LUCY KINSELLA (*contemporary British*)
'Rolling Horse' – bronze, signed and
numbered, Kinsella 2/4
*Provenance: Christie's, 20th century British
Art, 12.10.11*

DAME ELISABETH FRINK CH RA
(*British 1930-93*)
'Standing Man' – bronze, 1984, Ed. 4/4
Ref. SC15
Provenance: Beaux Arts Gallery

MARYANNE NICHOLLS
(*contemporary British*)
'The Vessel' – slate and fibreglass, 2005
Provenance: Piers Feetham Gallery, Aldeburgh

MICHAEL AYRTON RBA
(*British 1921-75*)
The Minotaur – bronze
*Provenance: Christie's, 20th century British
Art, Lot 118, 25.11.05*

LYNN CHADWICK CBE RA
(*British 1914-2003*)
'Two Watchers V'. Conceived 1967. Third
version – bronze, with grey patina
*Provenance: Christie's, 20th century British
Art, Lot 140, 4.6.04*

RONALD RAE (*contemporary British*)
Head of John the Baptist – granite
'The Wounded Elephant' – granite

Provenance: purchased from the artist

CATHY LEWIS (*contemporary British*)
'Salta 11' – bronze 7/9, 2001
'Continuum' – bronze 1/9, 2002
'Momentum' – bronze 4/9, 2002
Provenance: ex Anthony Hepworth, Bath

PHILIP JACKSON CVO FRBS
(*contemporary British*)
'Reading Chaucer' – bronze
Provenance: Portland Gallery, May 2009

NICOLA HICKS (*contemporary British*)
'Nice Little Earner' – bronze, numbered
and dated 'N.H. 8856'
*Provenance: Christie's, 20th century British
Art, Lot 166, 17.11.06*

DIDO CROSBY (*contemporary British*)
'Old English Billy Goat' – bronze 2003,
edition of six
Provenance: Csaky Art

ANGELA HUNTER
(*contemporary British*)
'Nanny Goat' – bronze resin, ed. 1/10
Provenance: Thompson Gallery, Aldeburgh

NORTH LAWN
JOHN M. BLASHFIELD (*British, active
1851–65*)
Garden Vase, on associated plinth –
terracotta

L. MIGNON (*French*)
Pair of Mastiffs – cast iron, 19th century
Provenance: Marché aux Puces, Paris

ROSE GARDEN
• Venetian Istrian stone wellhead,
decorated with lions' heads and foliage
• New ironwork by James Horrobin
created from a photograph of a wellhead in
a Venetian courtyard by Victor Edelstein
• A pair of 18th/19th century lead statues
of putti with Bacchic attributes, seated on
stone balls
• A pair of 19th century French bronze
groups of a Bacchante with tambourine

and putto beside her; and a gleaner with
a sheaf of corn slung on her back with a
putto beside her, reaching up for a gourd
(sulphated surfaces)

CENTAUR (*from the Antique*)
White marble

PAN PLAYING HIS PIPES (*from the
Antique*)
White marble

DIDO CROSBY (*contemporary British*)
'The Raven' – bronze
Provenance: purchased from the artist

ARABELLA LENNOX-BOYD
(*contemporary British*)
Oak Bench, with initials A (Anne) and M
(Michael) entwined on back support

SOUTH LAWN
GUY TAPLIN (*contemporary British*)
Large Cormorant – bronze, edition of 1/6,
1998. Large Preening Cormorant – bronze,
1/6, 1998
Provenance: ex London Zoo

ALISON CROWTHER
(*contemporary British*)
Cedar wood pine cones. Carved from the
wood of the magnificent old cedar tree
which once stood at the edge of the Spring
Garden, overhanging the lawn

**ALONG THE BORDER FROM
THE ROSE GARDEN TO THE
SWIMMING POOL**
• A set of four bronze cranes, 19th century
• A stone statue of Neptune at the far end
of the swimming pool
• A pair of Coade stone sphinxes, modern.
From Clifton Gardens
• Under a yew tree at the back of the
Summer House is a 19th century lead bust
of a Satyr playing pipes
• Under a further yew tree is a sculpture of
a swan – in limestone – flapping its wings
in rage, by Simon Winter